HARDPRESS.NET
HOME OF HARD-TO-FIND BOOKS

Blossomed Hours
by Edward Howard Griggs

Address:
HardPress
8345 NW 66TH ST #2561
MIAMI FL 33166-2626
USA
Email: info@hardpress.net

EDWARD HOWARD GRIGGS

Poetry (American)
American ? ..... . Misc.

LC

Grignon
NE

BLOSSOMED HOURS

Book of the Mind and Heart

BY
EDWARD HOWARD GRIGGS

ORCHARD HILL PRESS
Croton-on-Hudson
NEW YORK
1922

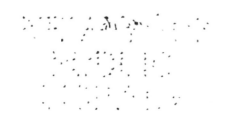

Copyright, 1922, by
EDWARD HOWARD GRIGGS

PRINTED IN U. S. A.

Rosemary, pansies, heart's-ease, rue:
  These are my garden flowers;
Memories, thoughts and responses true:
  These are my blossomed hours.

The Stuff of Dreams

[July 13, 1915]

MORE and more the drama of life grips one: the kaleidoscopic, incessantly moving stream of human beings, poured multitudinously forth from the prolific horn of Time, passing quickly across the film of life, into the dark and fathomless chasm of Eternity. Each unit in the innumerable throng living as if no other had ever been, tortured with heart-wrung agonies, lifted with wild hopes and desires, broken with thwarted dreams; yet ever driven swiftly on and away.

What does it mean—this passing spectacle of the stuff of dreams? Is it a transient shadow, cast on Immensity by a bewildered Mind? Is it the momentary revelation of Eternity on the screen of Time? All Thought ends in an unanswered question, to which only the Will replies.

Song

O THE lilt of music that words can carry,
    The lights and shadows that rise and
        fall,
The liquid lifting of sounds that marry
A deep heart's mood to the voice's call.

The gift of song is the key unlocking
All the doors to the inmost heart;
It can echo the wild sea's rocking,
The whisper of leaves in the wood apart.

Then weave the lyric of liquid measures,
Touch and waken the soul that sleeps;
Mingling in one the pains and pleasures
That brood in the spirit's ocean deeps.

[Glen Hill Farm, Twin Mountain, N. H., July 22, 1906]

NOTHING else is so barren as complete freedom for which one has no use. We chafe under bonds; but only through them does life get meaning. Every just limitation straightens the path we must travel, instead of leaving us to wander aimlessly in the forest. The one need is that we *travel the path*: when we do, every right restriction helps us go forward. Thus the sentimental yearning for an impossible freedom of caprice merely evidences weakness in meeting life's challenging opportunity.

TRUTH AND OPINION

[Vredeoord, Spuyten Duyvil, New York City, July 4, 1914]

AS, with the years, one gains wisdom, certain great truths of life come to lie permanently clear. One holds to these securely, as the basis on which to build conduct. The danger is that opinions also tend to become fixed, crystallizing into prejudice. The problem is, to cling firmly to fundamental convictions; yet avoid set opinions and pre-judgments, and hold one's whole philosophy of life subject to constant reformulation. The old man who, with age-long experience and reflection, keeps his mind open and responsive on every side and ever growing, is the true possessor of wisdom.

[Glen Hill Farm, August 10, 1909]

HOW life evades one! There is always the dream that the next step will bring the satisfying reality; but rarely indeed do the moments come when we are conscious that now we live completely. Even the wisest of us is subject to the delusion of somewhere else. If only we could change conditions a little, we think then we should live fully what we have dreamed; but the changes come and find us still anticipating. There is only one solution: *to live each moment*, to check longing and forego regret, to look before and after only to live the present to the full.

The Ship

THE thousand souls in the stately ship
    Sail silently into the west;
But the different moods that the thousand grip
No other could e'er have guessed.

For one went out with a heart aflame
With the dream of a fortune made,
And one was fleeing in terror and shame
From the shadow of love betrayed.

For untried scenes another sought,
That would give his mind relief;
With memories was another fraught
And shaken with lonely grief.

And one was a maiden, with dreams afire
Of the glory of life to be;
And one was a woman whose sad desire
Was only to rest in the sea.

But the ship sailed on with its human freight
In the path of the setting sun;
For life is the same for souls elate
And for those whose day is done.

[On train, Colorado, July 3, 1921]

THE young people of this generation have a difficult path to travel. They have freedom as never before, but less of religious foundation and guiding moral principles, even much less of social protection. Many will drift, some will slip and fall, there will be much waste of life; yet the fundamental instincts and eternal aspirations will dominate, and life will work forward, perhaps more swiftly because of the freedom.

CURRENT LITERATURE

[Vredeoord, Spuyten Duyvil, New York City, June, 1914]

MODERN sociological writings are poor, indeed, compared to literature; often pushing theories and formulas to the point of obscuring the very life they seek to interpret. How ephemeral is much that calls itself science; how eternal all insight into life.

On the other hand, most modern novels are sadly disappointing. One is constantly tantalized with the question whether the actions and situations are true, or even possible, in relation to the characters. Such a disconcerting doubt destroys the whole value of a work of art. An artist fails utterly unless he has the grasp of life and the compelling power in its portrayal which make the actions seem inevitable; absorbing the reader's attention, so that he is not turned back upon the disillusionizing doubt as to their possibility. One understands why the masters live and the others pass: it is not accident nor convention.

[Kansas City, Mo., June 15, 1921]

ONE should make an effort for constructive faith, instead of yielding to moods of pessimism and depression. Cheerfulness is a virtue that may be acquired, and it should be acquired, not only for the happiness of one's associates, but for the capital of one's own energy. Life is greatly determined by our moods; but our moods are, or *may be*, what we make them.

SCHNITZLER

[Chicago, November 22, 1920]

YES, the best of Schnitzler's work is powerful and beautiful, moving to tears with the spectacle of life, given at once with relentlessness and tenderness. It is not *all* of life, however; and there is a certain weak acceptance, in his free, self-affirming characters, that makes their tragedy inevitable.

The Lonely Way is the saddest of his dramas; and involves the most profound castigation of the refinedly selfish life. *The Intermezzo* is the tenderest; and Cecilia is one of the loveliest characters in modern literature. If only Amadeus, who deserved to do so, could have grasped her complete sincerity!

Over all, the chilling veil of tender sadness, fading the heart of desire in its inception and making vain the self-affirmation while it is willed! It is life, modern, tender, personal, sensuous; but it is not *all* of life.

Schnitzler's view is irony—gentle, tender but searching irony. There is an element of moral paralysis in the effect of it. Will it last in the modern spirit; or will the effect of the War be to sweep it away and create a more virile attitude, whether of doubt or faith?

14

[Tahlequah, Okla., June 18, 1921]

THE world has moved far from the positivism of Comte, George Eliot and Harriet Martineau. Doors, they had supposed closed forever, have quietly slipped open again; and we look up, surprised at new and old vistas revealed through them.

One cannot learn too deeply the lesson that the ideas of one's time, which seem so final, are but transient adjustments to a universe, vaster and more satisfying than all our views of it. Always there is truth in the dominant ideas of one's epoch; but never are they all the truth. It is right that we should discover and formulate them; but needful that we should hold them fluid, as merely temporary adjustments to life, that serve their day, but must pass or blend with other ideas, as we recognize more and other phases of the truth.

THE NEW AND THE OLD

[On Train, New Mexico, June 21, 1915]

THE old is new and the new is old. No novel conception will regenerate the world. Ideas that at first promise to transform society are found after awhile to have been expressed in the past, while the new factor is but a slight increment or a fresh combination of old elements. There is progress, but with a return in cycles of the rhythmic swing of life. It is hard to keep the balance between progress and repetition, appreciating at once the new and the old.

For instance: the "new" sociology, that applies fresh standards to life, is nearly all in Aristotle. Any sound ethics uses the same tests; and in attacking ethics the sociologists are setting up a straw adversary. So modern inductive science does not go far without using the same methods of reflection and interpretation it began by attacking.

Is it that to youth all is new; to age all is old; and each is half right, half wrong? Sanity, balance is the need: not the "golden mean" —which is usually anything but golden—but the *inclusive* view holding in relation the truth of both sides.

16

Nightfall

A LITTLE time of love and joy, with aspiration strong,
A world of hope and energy, with promises so
    high;
But quickly down the slope we pass, where
    stretch the shadows long,
For lark's song of the morning, sounds the
    whip-poor-will's weird cry.

The evening darkens, gray and chill, the silent
    curtain falls,
The bird that sang so loud at dawn sits quiet
    on the nest;
Through the leafage of the forest the dove no
    longer calls—
Let nature take her tired child to sleep upon
    her breast!

[Vredeoord, May 31, 1915]

THERE is a remarkably wise and detached spirit in Maeterlinck's *Wisdom and Destiny*—a philosophy worthy of Emerson; yet with an appreciation of personal passion and sorrow quite beyond Emerson. The book teaches a healthy gospel of happiness—though it be the Blue Bird that is everywhere and nowhere. Nevertheless, I draw back from any theory tending to hold the equivalency of all experience. There is tragedy that is dead loss, and joy that is unmixed life-gain. It is a peculiar mediocrity that would theorize away the tragic elements in great experience. Heroism shuts its teeth and takes them in their appalling deadliness. "Das Schicksal ist unerbittlich, und der Mensch wenig!" (Goethe's only remark to Voss on Schiller's last illness) is nearer the true attitude than is the spirit of *Wisdom and Destiny*.

Still, one bows to the loftiness of view, to the placing of wisdom above reason, to the high appreciation of the superiority of the soul to circumstances. The finest line in the book, which may be taken as the motto for all Maeterlinck's best work, is this: "He who sees without loving is only straining his eyes in the darkness."

MAETERLINCK is more the mystic, Emerson the intellectualist. Maeterlinck has saturated himself with phases of human experience, from which Emerson stood aloof. Both teach the soul: Emerson the soul of pure intelligence; Maeterlinck that of instincts, emotions and subtle appreciations.

WHAT IS INTELLIGENCE?

[State College, Pa., July 21, 1920]

TWO ants stop in the path, wave and cross their antennæ, then part and go severally about their tasks, having evidently exchanged information and arrived at intelligent decision.

What is intelligence? The mystery of mind is all there, as completely as in the highest reaches of human genius. What do we know? Our boasted science scratches a little on the surface, only to uncover fathomless deeps below. Mystery beyond mystery! Utter humility is the only wisdom.

[Edmond, Okla., June 15, 1915]

THE enthusiasm and energy of Western America are splendid. There is no chance there for the philosophy of despair. The West is the home of optimism.

When the country is all settled and the last generation of pioneers has passed: what then? It takes so little time for a civilization to grow settled and get the mood of age. It is evident in the eastern United States; and would be more so, were it not for the constant fertilization from the West.

After all, it is a poor faith that springs only from new environment and depends upon untilled soil. It is the faith, based on permanent elements of life, that age as well as youth can hold, which alone can furnish a lasting basis of civilization. Meantime, the West is the desirable field for the youth of this generation.

THE ROCKIES

[Moraine Lodge, Colorado, August 10, 1919]

WHAT a world this is: the meadow below in the foreground, and across and all around the circle of sublime mountains, jagged, irregular, glacier-torn, flinging their lofty summits to the sky. Glacial patches of snow and ice here and there, while below them is the sweep of spruce and pine forests. Many of the nearer isolated pines, fighting their centuries of battle with the storms, have been tempest-torn to tortured majesty. Forbidding, in bare and inaccesssible grandeur, the peaks lift away to their eternal communion with the winds and stars.

In our drive this morning, we climbed ever away from the far-sweeping valley, with forests on either side, above sheer gorges with falling streams, through deep stretches of blue and green spruce, fir and towering pines, ever toward the ragged and majestic ranks of serried crags, carved into war-blasted temples and naked spires, pointing sheerly to the blue dome of the sky.

The peace and solitude of these eternal mountains: how they rebuke the frivolous pettiness, the hot haste, the fevered struggle of

22

human life! A lifting above the submerging stream of events and incidents, calm and far perspective, a self-possession in the soul: it is these they give.

The Rocky Mountains

[From Moraine Park, August, 1919]

I

THE jagged peaks climb toward the sky's
  blue dome;
The sun shines down with hot intensity;
Deep forests, where untamèd beasts may roam,
Clothe all the lower slopes with density;
Summits, where Gods of Greece might find a
  home,
Loom, ice-torn symbols of immensity:
  Man ne'er can conquer the high mountain
    peaks,
  Where, 'mid the awful silences, God speaks.

II

Grandeur and majesty to lift the heart
Beauty in sombre trees to rest the eyes,
Ice patches whence the glacial waters start,
Swift leaping where the gleaming cataract flies;
Upon the rocks the tiny chipmunks dart,
At every turn the visions wide surprise:

24

How the eternal mountains lift one's life
Above the troubled world of human strife!

III

O'er the far peaks the storm clouds swift de-
    scend,
And sudden lightnings dart from cloud to
    cloud;
Across the sombre valley's rain-swept end
The echoing roll of thunder crashes loud;
The wakened pines beneath the tempest bend,
Then lift their century crests and straighten,
    proud:
    They sing the eternal music of the spheres—
    Earth's melody that fills the eyes with tears.

IV

As swiftly as it came, the rain doth cease;
The clouds rest softly on the mountain height;
The winds that laughed are still, and all is
    peace;
The western summits gleam with rosy light;
The high peaks, brightened with the storm's
    release,
Glow still, as o'er them soft descends the night;

While the full moon, in growing majesty,
Floods all the scene with light of mystery.

V

O what relief to weary heart and brain,
What blessèd peace the troubled spirit fills;
How Nature's grandeur heals the human pain,
And how her wondrous beauty wakes and
     thrills;
Lifting the spirit till it may attain
The majesty of the eternal hills:
     Three solitudes, to which the soul may flee—
     The desert, the high mountains and the sea!

[Kansas City, Mo., June 15, 1921]

TRUE moral, like intellectual, toleration is an index of fine and wide cultivation. The desire to regulate by law personal habits and conduct of life, in terms of mass opinion, is always a symptom of ignorant mediocrity. The kingdom of heaven will come by cultivation, not by legislation.

GREAT SALT LAKE

[Great Salt Lake, Utah, June 29, 1915]

OVER the wide semi-circle of the láke arches the dome of the sky: both cerulean blue; but the water thick, oily and translucent, the sky faintly luminous, with long stretches of gray-white clouds. Between lake and sky is the irregular line of gray-brown mountains, purpling with distant shadows. The air is hot, drying the nostrils. Over water and earth broods a sense of limitless desolation.

[Canyon, above Boulder, Col., August 17, 1920]

THIS mountain region is too overpowering in its bare and forbidding majesty. Great masses of rough rock, with red and yellow colors, straggling pines, huge hills rising behind: it is all positive, aggressive and startling in grandeur, never femininely beautiful and intimately appealing. The Westchester hills to live with!

The Rockies do not stimulate meditations and dreams as do our Eastern wooded mountains. They awaken activity, rather than foster repose. They will hardly create the thoughtful poetry born of the New England hills.

[Greeley, Colorado, July 31, 1918]

A LAND that must be irrigated always seems artificial, in spite of its luxuriance and its ceaseless sunshine. Its products, too, are unnaturally large, but lacking in the subtle flavors Nature ripens in her own way. Give me the land where the rain falls, the gray days rest the eyes and heart, and the clouds temper the sunshine to the mood of dreams!

Fulfillment

VOICES that ring with light laughter,
  And tones that are tender with pain:
Who knoweth what cometh after,
Nor why there is sunshine and rain?

Hearts that are burdened to breaking,
And eyes that are softened with love:
How strange is our life in the making,
With still-shining star-suns above.

In the morning the grass dew is sparkling,
For a little the sun is alight;
Then its shining is silenced to darkling
By the storm-clouds that deepen to night.

The path that was sweet in the forest
Goes on through a desert of rocks;
The lost joy gives pain that is sorest,
The hope that is broken but mocks.

[Ottawa, Canada, October 23, 1914]

DID Ibsen succeed in his early formed ambition to make his people "think great thoughts"? He made them think: that is certain; but there is a morbid element in the thinking, even in the far-reaching dreams, such as *The Master Builder* and *Rosmersholm.* One wonders about the net result of it all; but what a creator of men and women he is—"the eyes full of laughter, the throat of tears"!

His work has the quality of all masterpieces in growing on one steadily, as one rereads, and challenging thought ever more deeply as one reflects upon it. A perplexed and sombre giant, his masterpieces wrought out of doubt, pain and confusion, he towers above the modern pygmies, with his head in the threatening clouds.

[Vredeoord, July 21, 1914]

PEER GYNT is a strange feat of the imagination, with a wealth of dramatic energy, rollicking incident and wild fantasy, and unlike any other poem in the world. Was Ibsen, under the influence of Italy, giving wild rein to his imagination and freeing himself from his northern inheritance, as Goethe, in lesser degree, did in the Witches' Kitchen scene in *Faust?*

A type, partly Norwegian, but in the main universally human, Peer Gynt represents fantasy substituted for reality, and selfish whim in place of self-realization. Wanting consistent strength, he descends to evanescent brawling; for steady growth, he substitutes mere change of scene and action. Thus he becomes the hill Troll, whose sordid and selfish maxim, "To thyself be enough" replaces the impersonal human ideal, "Become thyself"—grow into the fullness of thine own potential life.

So all the wide wanderings, restless incidents, ceaselessly varied scenes, activities and experiences end in—nothing—dross for the moulder's ladle. To have stayed in the hut with Solveig would have been life: *that* was the forfeited kingdom!

[Atlanta, Georgia, April 15, 1914]

STRANGE, and indicative of Ibsen's long and slow development, that the series of great stage dramas, which won for him an international audience and by which he is generally remembered, was produced entirely after he was fifty years old. *The Doll's House* opens the series and explains his victory. It is, indeed, a masterpiece, powerfully moving dramatically; its characters, not puppets or caricatures, but living human beings, with all the motives and emotions of actual life. Has there appeared a greater and finer appeal for the true emancipation of women? The birth of the charming kept girl into the self-affirming, self-directed woman is one of Ibsen's noblest achievements.

Ghosts perhaps represented a step backward, overdoing somewhat the heredity notion, that afflicted the late nineteenth century; but in comparison with more recent plays exploiting sex and disease, it stands out in impressive and elevated dignity. Its strength, moreover, lies in uniting the two types of ghosts—the biological and the social. Had it not been for false conceptions of duty—ghosts of the past—accentuated by the conventional pastor, the biological curse could not have been perpetuated. It was thus social convention, not blind heredity, that forced the woman back and insisted that the sins of the father should be visited on

33

the children. Even here, Ibsen is the constructive teacher, unmasking false convention and hypocritic living to appearances, and revealing what freedom and truth may accomplish in removing evils, though inherent in the natural process of life.

[Vredeoord, May 8, 1914]

ROSMERSHOLM is no less impressive than when first read, twenty years ago. The majesty of the moral order of the universe when one stands naked before it: that the drama reveals with compelling power. Here, as always, however, Ibsen is more inexorable than life. Since Rebecca West *is* transformed by love, there is something else before her, besides the mill-race; and Rosmer, wakened out of his weak blindness, should go forward with the woman who is truly his mate, in her virtues as in her faults. Life is not in dreaming over great causes nor vainly brooding over changeless yesterdays: Rosmer should turn from both, to build what is possible from the broken fragments of life that remain.

EVEN more than *Rosmersholm, Hedda Gabler* is realism, but with the difference Ibsen gives to everything his genius touches. The characters are dreamed out to completion, instead of being copied from fragmentary actuality.

The incarnation of sensitive egotism, Hedda Gabler is too selfish to give herself to a grand passion or a great aim. Without the big interests, of which her nature might otherwise have been capable, with the boring vacancy of her inner life, she lets herself follow capricious whims and becomes petty and perversely cruel.

Tesman is too entirely the weakling: even a little man will sometimes flash fire. In fact, the flame is apt to be intense, in proportion as the nature is habitually weak.

Judge Brack is too coldly and consistently the villain; Mrs. Elvsted, too purely the redeeming inspiration; yet when all is said, how the play grips with its vital dramatic power and its impression of inevitableness in every character and situation: *that* is Ibsen!

[Greenville, South Carolina, April 9, 1914]

LITTLE EYOLF, even more than *The Master Builder* and equally with *When We Dead Awaken*, represents the symbolic type of Ibsen's work. Rita is the one healthily human character, excepting the slightly-drawn engineer, stronger and really finer than anyone else in the play. In disagreement with the critics, I find her a very lovable woman, born to be comrade and mate, rather than mother.

Alfred is the weak dreamer, pushed to the point that he ceases almost to have human reality. His brooding over the never-written masterpiece on "Human Responsibility," while neglecting equally his duties and opportunities as husband and father, is too transparently didactic a symbol. His aspiration toward the high mountains and "great waste places" is like Ibsen's taciturn brooding apart.

The weird Rat Wife, luring "all creeping and crawling things," is a nightmare symbol; while it is evident what Little Eyolf and Asta represent.

The oblivion of Alfred's spiritual egotism is far worse than Rita's frankly human selfishness. One feels that she will expiate, really caring for the poor children she takes to her house and heart; while Alfred will resent their noise and presence, and go on dreaming of something else in the great waste places of his soul. It is a pity Rita could not have bought a better lover with her "gold and green forests"!

There is a certain unreality in it all. In life, Little Eyolf does not fall from the table just in the hour of ecstasy of Alfred and Rita, nor does he drown at the moment of his mother's half-expressed wish that he did not stand between her husband and herself.

Was it that Ibsen's long, silent brooding apart made his characters too much figments of the imagination, lacking something of the complicated reality of actual men and women? Events, after all, do not occur in real life with the ironic consistency of Ibsen's plots.

Life is at once more complex and more simple than in Ibsen: more complex because a greater variety of tendencies is evident in any person; more simple, in that Ibsen's relentless carrying to conclusion of the dominant quality in each character results in a complicated situation that life would relieve.

The truth of Ibsen is thus, in a totally different modern way, not unlike that of Dante. As Dante isolates the one fact of sin or virtue, and shows its final consequence in the soul of the doer, so Ibsen takes one leading trait or tendency of character, and develops its complete working out in life. In this he is idealist as much as realist.

[St. Catharine's, Canada, October 24, 1914]

NO one has interpreted the awakening and world-wide restlessness of modern women as has Ibsen. Perhaps that is one reason his women are so superior to his men. What a collection of cads and weaklings his men are! Dr. Stockmann and certain of the physicians are kindly, it is true. Brand is a towering exception, but he is distorted and half-mad—far below his mate; while the women: Nora, Ellida, Agnes, Solveig, Maia, Irene, Rita, Hilda Wangel, Rebecca West, even Hedda Gabler: all had great and lovable capacities for life. Is the contrast due to the new interest of the age, as of Ibsen, in the awakened woman's problem; so that men are

38

portrayed as a dramatic background, against which the vivid feminine rôles are played out?

[Vredeoord, May 28, 1914]

COMPARED with Goethe, Ibsen's life seems singularly narrow and perhaps unfulfilled. They utterly misunderstand Goethe, who think he cultivated love-affairs as material for his art. He *lived* his experiences; and *afterwards* searched his own past for material and insight in his art. Much the same seems to have been Ibsen's relation to the late ray of sunshine that warmed his waning life. He lived the experience (O without violating any social convention) and for a time it was too tender and poignant for him to wish to express it in art: afterwards, it gave him *The Master Builder*.

The development of Goethe's genius was much more genial and natural than was that of Ibsen's. A true artist from the beginning, Goethe responded easily, growing naturally through the series of influences playing upon him. Ibsen forced his genius by sheer, persistent, dominating effort. Thus at an age when much of Goethe's great work was already achieved, Ibsen first completely found himself and began his series of truly independent masterpieces: the spectacle is amazing.

Did Ibsen ever come to clear faith? To the end, he seems groping through confused mists; but recognizing with growing clearness a few fundamental ideas as the basis of life. Truth, love, freedom, the unceasing affirmation of the will: these are the principles that gradually emerge in his thought, as the foundation on which all life must rest. The applications, however, are far from clear. Ibsen points the way, but sees not the issue, except in half-despairing dreams. That he is so great an interpreter of the modern world is a searching criticism upon that world.

[Bowling Green, Ky., April 21, 1914]

WHAT a sum of confused contradictions Ibsen is; satyr and priest, cynic worldling and flaming preacher, Mephistopheles and Jeremiah, hard realist and symbolic dreamer, now using coldly the anatomist's knife in dissecting the evils of modern society, now bend-

40

ing to sing lyric songs with all the tenderness of a loving woman.

An intense egoist, Ibsen regarded his talents as a supreme impersonal obligation. Struggling ever forward for liberty of mind and spirit, he was a conservative in politics, pouring out scorn on most of the movements of modern democracy. He was apparently capable of warm friendships with intellectual comrades, and seems to have been a good husband and father; yet he separated himself from his parents for twenty years, not caring even to write. A social revolutionist, he delighted in orders and decorations. Scorning the timid, frugal virtues of Norway, he was a thrifty saver and a shrewd investor. Loving ease and luxury, responding almost as a sybarite when they came, he starved through decades and fought through others with the grim specter of poverty ever at the door. Passionately hungering for success, he endured hate, misunderstanding and abuse for many years.

He did not fully reap the spiritual fruit of his sufferings; nor did he yield and win fortune by time-serving compromise. No, he flung back the challenge with added hate, and forced the attacker into the defense. He is ever the ice Jötun of the North, ready to flame into the Loki of scourging fire.

Balanced sanity, cosmopolitan wisdom, harmony and serenity: these are Shakespeare and Goethe, not Ibsen. A revolutionist, like Whitman, he is at the opposite extreme from that believing optimist. His silence was fierce brooding, not serene meditation; his solitude was Titanic, not Olympian. What a mocker he is; but a grave, tragic mocker, not the gay maker of Gallic persiflage. He is a great but marred Titan; a Goethe fallen on evil days and groping among the shadows; an earnest preacher, but sadly unsure of his sermon, and sick—O with the mortal sickness of modern life! Failure, tragic failure is at the end in almost everything he has written; with here and there a little alleviating gleam that makes the darkness seem blacker; and the ever-recurring aspiration toward the summits: what are they, but the desolate rocks of ice-clad peaks, silent with the peace of death!

Dejection

THE wind is still, the sun is set,
  The last light lingers on the walls;
My heart is torn, my eyes are wet,
The mourning doves coo ceaseless calls.

The shadows deepen on the grass,
The trees draw up in sombre gloom;
The hopes that seemed so fair, alas!
Are withered like late autumn's bloom.

O heart that aches with bitter pain,
O tired eyes and weary hands,
O mind that sought the ends proved vain—
The path is lost amid the sands!

[Greeley, Col., July 31, 1918]

IF this chapter were all of life, what a strange, ironic jest it would be.

I stepped on three caterpillars hurrying at intervals across the walk. Each moving with all its might, seeking food and the place to weave a cocoon, I suppose: striving toward its destiny.

Stepped upon, they were little spots of ugly matter, swiftly drawn into the blind inorganic mass. Where went the sentient, psychical life, so feverish in conscious activity a moment before?

[Grand Canyon of the Colorado, 6 A. M., June 22, 1915]

TO the East the abyss is misty darkness, with shadowy cathedrals dimly hinted in the mysterious gloom. To the West stretches away the irregular chasm, lighted by the early sun: tier on tier of heterogeneous and receding palisades—red, yellow, brown and gray; piled upon these, ten thousand Aztec and Egyptian temples, doorless and windowless, deserted for æons, crumbling in barbaric desolation; while over all is the radiant and cloudless blue, with the intense light deepening the colors and shadows.

HOW small Man seems beside the tortured splendor of this gigantic abyss. What sudden convulsions of Nature to lift these strata, what ages upon ages to cut them down and carve them into tortuous temples of the pagan Gods!

It is as if Nature had combined here all the towering and colossal forms she carves in the mountains of this Western wilderness, and then had painted them with all the colors, the lights and shadows, she creates from stone and soil, from sun and air.

45

Titanic temples, eternal, but crumbling in colossal ruin, with the wild cry of the pine-trees behind; primeval desolation under transfiguring light; abysmal chaos moulded to mysterious and haunting forms; an infernal urge of creation caught and crystallized in an eternal moment just before the cosmos is born: how the human imagination staggers under the overpowering weight of demonic majesty!

NOW, in the late afternoon, it is the East chasm and towering walls that stand revealed in bare splendor; while the Western gulf, with far-thrown battlements stretching into it, is withdrawing into the mystery of ever-deepening shadows. It reaches away and away: the sense of space multiplied; the grandeur growing, as the embattled temples recede and shroud themselves in purple haze.

One more point rounded, and now the Eastern basin rises through dull red battlements to lavender walls, topped with gray. The *silence*—broken only by the rising and falling moan of the pines! The dominant impression, that of primeval desolation—even as

46

chaos when God first said, "Let there be light"!

O WILDERNESS of weird forms, tortured into veiled symbols of all that Man has dreamed and done: what eternity ye combine with what everchanging beauty of color, shape and shadow! How transient, Man's temples, beside the rock-firm permanence of your brooding domes! The falling rain-drops and the soft-moving waters leave no trace; but the æonian flood here sculptures what no gigantic engine could build, no swift-passing human hand achieve. Mysterious Nature, silent-moving, mighty Mother of life: all the Titan tortures of your God-kissed breast stand here revealed in rebuking majesty and wordless speaking grandeur to the fall of Time!

[On train, California, June 28, 1915]

A WORLD of memories, and of how large and significant a chapter of life: such is this Western land to me. At once, the chapter seems so near and so far away. A palimpsest is the spirit, written over and over; and all the texts are there, layer below layer. If one seems forgotten, there is needed but some renewed association—the acid of this sunlight—and it stands clear and legible, as if just written with the iron pen of experience.

A Love Song

O FLOWER with a beauty transcending,
  Charming the sight;
O Lily, all loveliness blending,
  Rose of delight!

O Heart of a thousand surprises,
  Lips of desire;
O Eyes in which love-light arises,
  Spirit of fire!

Thy voice hath a melody thralling,
  Hauntingly low;
As tenderly o'er the heart falling
  As windless snow.

Thy life to all beauty is glowing,
  Heart of a flame;
My spirit with joy is o'er-flowing,
  Breathing thy name.

THE PANAMA EXPOSITION

[San Francisco, June 26–28, 1915]

THE Exposition is beautiful, beyond all one had been led to expect: masses of dull colors—red, pink, blue, buff, gray, green; a multitude of stately colonnades—somewhat over-decorated; a wealth of Spanish towers and low domes, with wind-blown banners copied from the olden time. The whole is like a Moorish dream, called into momentary being under this radiant sky, and in deep harmony with the tawny hills.

It is fortunate to experience the wonder of the Grand Canyon and of this man-made marvel in such close succession. Both impress with the bewildering wealth of colors and of forms; but in such widely different fashion. *There* was chaos, caught in an eternal moment of creation; here is a human cosmos of finished forms, but with an impression of artifice and so pitifully transient. Man rises far above and beyond Nature; but how ephemeral is his life and much of his achievement.

What a pity it seems that so vast an expenditure of wealth should be for a purpose so temporary. If but a fraction of the money could be used in rebuilding a few beautiful structures in San Francisco! Since the city could summon such taste to the erection of these impermanent palaces, is it not strange that her buildings should be so ugly—worse even than before the Earthquake?

THE supreme artistic merit of the Exposition is its wonderful harmony, unifying nearly all the structures, their applied colors, and associated sculpture and shrubbery, in one unified impression of beauty. In this it is immeasurably more beautiful than the St. Louis Fair and far outrivals the White City at Chicago. No preliminary description prepared one for this surprise, amazing in the light of the wealth and variety of colors used. Jules Guérin, who planned and carried out the entire color scheme, has proved himself one of those rare great masters, able to execute in perfect harmony the bewildering detail embodying all aspects of a grandiose dream.

The new medium used in the walls—a combination plaster and stucco, imitating the soft-toned Travertine stone—carries an imposing sense of massive strength for buildings so unlasting. At a little distance it gives the impression of the small Roman bricks, while the texture lends itself to the warm dull hues.

FESTIVAL Hall and the Horticultural Building are the two false notes in the main group of structures. The green pointed domes—one lantern-topped—disagree with the square towers, low Moorish domes and round arches of the other buildings. Fortunately, the two stand at one side.

The Tower of Jewels is somewhat garish. Too broad in the base, the impression of its height is inadequately given; while the "jewels" might have been spared. At night, however, when illuminated, whether from without by the intense white light, or from within with the soft red glow, it takes its rightful place.

THE plan of a series of partially enclosed courts is peculiarly attractive in this climate and with the location exposed to the constant winds. In every court one can find a protected corner, in sun or shadow as the comfort of the hour demands, where one can sit and dream, with the vistas of beauty on every hand.

Such a sheltered nook is this west portico of the Court of Flowers: open at the south and flanked by two impressive towers; closed on the north by a circular portico; the columns buff touched with green; the inner walls dull red, with lavender gray below; in the foreground, solid masses of yellow pansies, with lines of green shrubbery. The sun plays magic with the soft colors, so that the tones change from hour to hour, but always in harmony. The green columns in the towers form the only questionable note in the color scheme.

The variety within the unity is endless: the Court of the Four Seasons, in restrained style, with unfluted, buff Ionic columns and dark red pilasters, its four fountains flanked by soft pink walls; the rectangular Florentine and Venetian courts, decorated with Robbia-like plaques in blue and white, and reliefs upon the columns, are satisfying examples.

FOR an hour, I have been sitting by the lagoon, across from the open rotunda before the Fine Arts building. The soft red dome against the luminous blue sky, over the gray reliefs on a buff ground; the dark-veined Corinthian columns below; the swinging semi-circles of buff and gray arcades at either side; the brown water in the foreground; the low walls covered with blossoming moss across: all unite in an impression of majesty softened with beauty.

The suggestion of picturesque and romantic ruins is given, without being carried too far, in this circular sweep of the Fine Arts building, with the detached peristyles and domed arches before it. This series of structures is the masterpiece of the Exposition. Each step one takes gives changing vistas of beauty. The shrubbery has been used here with consummate skill, fitted to the walls as if growing for centuries, adding to the sense of age and romantic association. The irregular lagoon is the crowning element in the changing beauty of the whole. Had the art of the Exposition achieved nothing else than this one series of harmonies it would have been amply justified.

THE best of the art collection is in the bronzes and marbles scattered artistically amid the shrubbery, between the peristyles and the Art building. The collection within the building, on the whole, is mediocre, with a few beautiful works among the mass. It is remarkable how few great landscapes are in the collection. Does this mean a turning away from landscape work in current art?

AT times, the decoration is too flamboyant, but in the main it is in harmony with the joyous beauty of the general plan. The *modern* character of the sculptures—often in theme and generally in treatment—is particularly striking. It is surprising, but satisfying, to find, in the Court of Abundance, the ages of Man treated on the basis of Darwinian evolution, and not on that of conventional classic tradition, with a successful impressiveness that well illustrates the possibilities for art in the modern world view.

Brangwyn's Four Elements are the most satisfying of the exterior frescoes. Strong in color, simple in symbolism, vigorous rather than delicate in form, wholly modern in the treatment of an ancient theme: they are admirable.

The Rising Sun and the Descent of Night, in beauty and immediate suggestiveness, are the loveliest of the symbolic sculptures. The one, a vigorous masculine figure, alive with up-springing aspiration; the other of delicately moulded feminine beauty, shrinking with exquisite sensitiveness into the silence: they carry the mood of the day and the night.

To these must be added the detached masterpiece, The End of the Trail: in sad tenderness, the most sympathetic interpretation of the vanishing red man ever achieved.

IT is less the spirit of California, the Exposition carries as its dominant impression, than the most cosmopolitan genius of the United States, *interpreting* the spirit of California. That is what lifts the whole from the sectional mood and makes it a universal artistic achievement. It is a crowning illustration of America's power to accept all the past, assimilate, use and enjoy it; yet live upon it with fresh virility today. Herein is the promise in a war-torn world.

One scarcely knows whether the whole is more beautiful by day, in the radiant sunshine and against the intense blue of the sky, or at night in the changing wonder of the illumination. Then the fairy-land impression is accentuated, while the indirect lighting brings out new glowing beauties, and the search lights reveal the higher sculptures. The softened glow gives no sense of garish artificiality, but rather an impression of the momentary transfiguration of the wondrous forms of a dream.

FAREWELL, O beautiful Dream—birth of an imagination as creative as the Nature that paints these hills with tawny gold and makes luminous the blue dome of the sky! Your transient temples will crumble, your domed arches and stately colonnades will fall; but your soul will live in hearts gladdened with beauty and minds chastened by sublimity to reverence and awe. How you lift away and rest one from the horror of a world aflame with war! That you can be—even momentarily—in such an epoch, is hope and faith to look across this sorrowful time to the better that is to be!

[August 23, 1920]

WHAT ceaseless effort is necessary to achieve and maintain success in any field. A thousand are watching and eager to jump into the place of any one who falls by the way. In intellectual work, competition goes on, keyed to the same fierce point. Must it not always be so, to get good work done? If this is true of the highest work, where the incentive is so largely in the task itself, must it not be true in more material fields? Therefore, are not those who seek to eliminate competition striking at the very vitals of life?

THE THINKER'S TASK

[Vredeoord, May 28, 1915]

ONE must strive incessantly never to let the desire to influence affect the effort to understand. The highest intellectual aim is to know and record reality.

The thinker must free himself from all limitations of his time and place, and strive to see as far forward as possible, in order to announce the line of progress. To be the seer, he must not fear the highest nor consider overmuch the adaption of his thought to the conditions of his age.

Did She But Know

NOVEMBER skies of blue and gray
  Hang over low;
A quiet, hazy, chilly day,
  Earth white with snow.

As is the day, my heart is chill,
  I wander slow.
With restless pain I murmur still
  "Did she but know!"

My rambles give no pleasure now,
  Alone I go.
She knows not that I suffer—how
  Then could she know?

Could she but see how torn the heart
  That suffers so;
Could she but feel its bitter smart,
  Did she but know:

Within my heart without a tear
  I'd bury woe;
Could she but whisper to me, "Dear,
  I feel and know!"

HUMAN WRECKAGE

[New York City, June 11, 1911]

IN the late afternoon of the hot Saturday, we sat on the bench in the Forty-second street park, behind the Public Library. All round us was the débris of a great city: homeless vagabonds, sodden featured, in frayed, dirty clothes, huddled upon the benches, seizing the opportunity for sleep. One whiskey-soaked girl—a slav apparently—with heavy, flat feet, reddened face, dirty shoddy garments and hat awry, lolled forward upon the seat.

A half-crazed woman, with dried and colorless face, carrying a huge Bible under her arm, walked slowly from group to group, muttering "You must be born again; you must be born again."

Cabs containing weazened-faced babies were pushed over the hot asphalt walks by tired and bedraggled women. Toward the library, little children, with something of the irrepressible happiness of their years, tossed balls or chased the sparrows. A mountainous, misshapen old woman sank together, like a telescope, on one of the benches. An aged and broken clergyman walked tremblingly by, leaning on the arm of his middle-aged daughter; sat a moment to rest; then struggled to his feet and moved painfully on.

Saddened and questioning, we wandered away, returning an hour later. A slight rain had intervened; and the benches were empty. Where had it gone—that human wreckage: To miserable lodgings, back rooms of saloons, protecting doorways? Like a morbid moving-picture, it had passed, leaving the empty screen.

WHAT a mocker Voltaire was, yet as one reads him more widely, the impression of his underlying sincerity grows steadily. The mockery is in the method, while the aim is earnest. How keenly he saw through the intellectual and social follies of his time, and scathingly scored them! He was the Erasmus of his age—only more mocking and less constructive, as the age was more vicious and superficial. After Erasmus came the Reformation; after Voltaire, the Revolution. One wonders whether satire ever works a thoroughgoing cure. Apparently not in vicious epochs; yet these especially invite it. The world is wide enough for all types of men and method; but one comes back to quietly constructive work as the only kind always helpful and never hurtful at all.

VOLTAIRE'S *Mémoires* of his stay in Berlin tell the whole story of the Hohenzollerns. Frederick the Great—absolute autocrat, unscrupulous, vain, treacherous, selfish— is the family model.

One gets a sense here, as in his novels, that Voltaire, in spite of his vanity and occasionally salacious mockeries, was a tolerant, broad, just modern mind, working with a mingling of rash boldness and reluctant prudence for the emancipation of the mind and spirit. I am surprised at the measure of essential reverence there is in him.

Wonderful Eighteenth Century! Is it possible our world may be trembling on the brink of revolution, as was Voltaire's, all unknown to him?

Erasmus

[At Bâle, Switzerland, a Winter evening, in February, 1523]

IN this ill-smelling, student's room I sit
　　And shiver, leaning against the monstrous
　　　　stove,
That vainly radiates deceptive warmth;
Without, the circle of bleak mountain slopes,
While streets of Bâle are piled feet deep with
　　　　snow.
　　Why did I not accept Pope Julius' gift,
And stay at Rome, to drink his mellow wine
And eat his ortolans?　A sunny land,
Much honor, easy wealth had then been mine.
But no, I must away, to wander wide,
Through France and Holland, England, Ger-
　　　　many;
Settling at last in this bleak, icy land,
To write with fingers numb, and drink sour
　　　　wine,
With brain befuddled by the musty air!
　　Why did I do it—I who have no taste
For martyrdom, but love the things of earth—

The luxuries and comforts of the flesh?
   It was a power stronger than my desires:
A driving love of freedom, and a sense
Instinctive of a mission to this age—
To shock men out of lethargy, and laugh
Their shallow forms and dry beliefs to scorn;
That so a true enlightenment might be,
A culture that should unify in one
The learning and the art of classic times
With character and conduct like to Him
Who preached upon the mount in Galilee.
That was my dream: that thus the world might
         be,
And so the church, remoulded from within.
   But Luther came, and broke my half-won
         hope,
Plunging the world again into a storm
Of controversy over sacraments
And mediæval doctrines, best unknown.
   Yet what a man!   How fearlessly he smote
With Saxon broad-ax at the root of ills
As old as man.   While I, with mocking smile,
And slender rapier of irony,
Sought but to fence with clumsy fools, and
         pierce
The paper breast-plate of their prejudice.

Was his the way, or mine?   I wonder oft;
But his way was not mine, and cannot be.
For he has set the whole world by the ears,
Destroyed the slowly fostered humanism,
Stirred up a mess; and I, in my old age,
Like to a mouse caught in a pitch-pot, strive
In vain to extricate my work and self.
Pope Adrian bids the crab to fly to Rome
And write against the Lutherans; while they
Attack me, since I cannot join their sect.
I stand between, berated by both sides.
Best is, I wrap me in a cloak of scorn
For both antagonists, and go my way—
A lonely way—and let them fight it out;
In hope than when enough of both are slain,
The controversial smoke may draw away;
And in a later age men may arise,
Who love the simple Christian character,
The solid learning of antiquity
And all the arts that grace the life of man.
There is no other hope; so let it be:
Reluctantly a martyr, I must wait,
And hope that some day all I sought to do
Will be made clear, and all my many books,
Swift writ, with pungent satire for the hour,

Will then be read as prophecies of light
And heralds of that better world to be.
   Another glass of this sour wine, and then
To sleep!

INTELLECTUAL BALANCE

[July 21, 1920]

TIMES for quiet meditation rest the spirit immeasurably. It is a pity to drive the mind too constantly—almost as much as to have its energies dissipated with constantly changing impressions. Stimulus, concentration, repose: it is the balance of these three factors that makes sane, productive mental life.

[Vredeoord, June 3, 1915]

THERE is in the universities a prejudice against teaching. A college professor feels even ashamed of the reputation of teacher. It is "original research" for which he would be famed—a fine thing in its place, but totally different from teaching. The result is, the poorest teaching to be found anywhere is in the universities. The philanthropist who wants to make a novel contribution should endow a college whose function is merely to teach.

THE radicals who will accept nothing, unless they can have everything and have it their own way, hamper real progress. Since all social adjustments are among human beings, each step must be a compromise; and no change, however important, can create an ideal social order.

Let any one of the radical proposals be accepted, such as the abolishing of private ownership of land: as long as many people are greedy and lazy, greed and laziness would find ways of expression. Reckless spawning would still produce population pressure. Men of superior energy would find ways of getting more land to till and securing others to work for them—those with insufficient initiative, foresight and thrift to till land for themselves —and so group subordination would be back again.

Equally hampering are those who can see progress only in replacing political by industrial organization of society. Politics is only a name: there is as much of it in labor unions as in the existing state. Demagoguery, selfish ambition, mob thinking and action would appear as fully under an economic, as under the present political organization of society.

Those who view all reforms, except their own specific, as mere palliatives, are the real obscurantists and enemies of progress, no matter what name they assume. Every step counts, as in the past every step has counted; and even palliatives are most desirable when pain is acute.

One wearies, too, of the ceaseless demand for reform: the thousand specifics loudly proclaimed, each as the certain cure-all. Meanwhile, the great world rolls on: men sinning and loving, suffering and strugglihg, as of old. "Why so hot, little men!" God has waited a long time; we, too, must wait. To work hard at the task, and not hope overmuch: that is wisdom.

[On train, Nebraska, June 30, 1915]

THE bare, rocky mountains and wide stretches of sand waste have given way to long reaches of green fields. The sky is softer blue, less intense and luminous. Rebuking majesty is replaced by a more genial human mood.

Everywhere the luxuriant vegetation encroaches upon the desert. Whether this be due to a natural change of climate or to human activity—the planting of trees and tilling the soil—certainly the green moves ever westward; so that one feels little of the desert will, in the end, remain unconquered.

Dark summer rain clouds gather above the wide stretches of fertile fields: how different from the far western landscapes. The relentless sunshine and brilliant sky of California challenge and stimulate with bold beauty; but they do not rest nor incite to quiet meditation. Each aspect of Nature has its own beauty and appeal. Clouds may tower, even as mountains, with a compensating majesty for these wide-rolling plains.

[June 29, 1919]

THE *Mémoires* of the period of Louis XIV and XV—Saint-Simon and so many others—take one over into another world, strangely remote and seeming unreal. The aristocrats, living their life of amusement, etiquette, intrigue, sycophancy, dissipation, took it with great seriousness, never doubting that it was the only important existence in the world. One would scarcely know that there were any other people in France: they are mentioned once in a hundred pages.

Wars of succession, of intrigue, for territory and glory; envious plotting of bed-chamber politics; John Law and his paper money scheme, raising many to apparent wealth for a few weeks, with the colossal crash following; all the time the people underneath suffering, starving, muttering; the Revolution drawing ever nearer, while the aristocrats never dreamed that their existence was not to be eternal, or that their "divine right" could ever be questioned: it all has profound warning for the bourgeois aristocracy of wealth today.

Our situation is in no way comparable to that of seventeenth and eighteenth century

France; but it takes far less arrogance and in-
justice to produce revolution now than then.
If we do not swiftly grant the justice in ad-
vance and educate the spirit of living in har-
mony with the good of all, we shall see the
capitalist class swept into the vortex, in the
throes of a far more complete revolution than
that of the 18th century; and then, what?
Who knows?

That we shall have revolution is not likely.
The awakening of a sense of conscious re-
sponsibility to one's fellows, of the sincere de-
sire to achieve justice for all, promises to work
out a peaceful and progressive solution; but
the other ominous alternative is there, looming
ever more threatening. Those with wealth
and power in their hands would better recog-
nize in time that arrogance, privilege, extrav-
agance and selfish indulgence pave the shortest
road to destructive revolution.

Italy Calls

OVER the swell of the sea and the play
of its waters,
Over the crest of the waves with their rhyth-
mic curling,
Kissed by the countless lips of the sea that
loves her,
Italy calls!

Soft as a breath of wind in the pines of Ra-
venna,
Faint as the kiss on the lips of Angelico's
angels,
Tender as sighs that utter the sorrow of Dante,
Italy croons:

"Come, O child of mine, though a northern
born exile;
Thine is the sun that shines with luxuriant
splendor,
Thine is the sky that glows with a light tran-
scendent—

Come, O Come!"

And O, my Beloved, let us listen the heart-
waking summons,
Come, O Come, let us go to the land of de-
sire,
Where brooding with bountiful blessings of
love and of beauty
Italy waits!

Away from the care and the discord of mis-
understanding,
Away from the aimless hurry of feet unresting,
Away from the pitiless pain of the long separa-
tion,
My Belovèd, O Come!

She will accept us—land of the sea and the
mountains,
Free as the wind that wakens the song in her
pine-trees,
Warm as the color that crimsons her countless
paintings—
Land of desire!

O Come! She will welcome us, Sweet, to some
  Apennine village,
Where mouldering churches glow with angelic
  madonnas
And babies, sweet as the children that troop
  in her meadows,—
   She whispers us, "Come!"

[Florence, Italy, July, 1907]

WHAT a world of art Florence is! Each dim church with its grave aisles and lofty nave, each street corner with its madonna niche, each rough-hewn but strongly majestic palace, vies with the bewildering wealth of gallery paintings in impressing one that here art springs from the very soil and is alive in the instinct of every Florentine.

How impressive the Cathedral: the great columns lift away, the space is multiplied in vastness, the dim light, sifting through the stained windows, gives a sense of mystery; while behind the altar, under the huge dome, in the late afternoon, the unfinished last work of Michael Angelo gives, as it were, the key note to the solemn impression of the whole. How little priest or people understand the lofty past behind them: it lifts itself away in solemn reserve from the careless multitude.

How sweet and childlike the soul of Luca della Robbia must have been; and what joy to let that soul blossom out—almost without effort—to the delight of the art-loving populace. Strange that a time of incessant and restless strife should have produced such simplicity and childlike response to life. It but shows again how all man is in each of us; and any aspect will blossom forth when opportunity and appeal come.

Gone—all gone!—Andrea's lonely hunger and Botticelli's impoverished old age; the tragic struggles of gigantic Angelo and Raphael's popularity and short-lived joy; the high ambition of Brunelleschi and the fame of Giotto; Savonarola's hope and agony; the battles of Blacks and Whites in the streets of Florence; the woe of world-wandering Dante and the aspirations of Angelico—gone, all gone! Wait a little, and you too! Ah, but there is no hope or comfort in that—the answer must be deeper, if life is sane.

Sunset At Assisi

LIGHT fleece clouds over all the heavens
    unrolled,
Softly the sun behind the hills doth slip,
Till all the clouds are swift aflame with gold,
That turns to red, warm as a maiden's lip;
Then fades to dimmer hues, till gray and cold,
The color dies away from each cloud tip;
    Till in the heaven the myriad stars shine,
        still,
    While o'er the heart descends the night air
        chill.

It seemed so sad—the splendid holocaust
That Nature offered up to God above—
Should thus in night and nothingness be lost;
Like all the tender, cherished things we love:
Spring star-flowers in the woodland thicket
        mossed
And all the joyous hours we reck not of:
    But in the soul that beauty still survives,

For it had touched and changed our inmost
    lives.

E'en thus with men who come from out the
      night
And pass across this transient scene of things:
They have their little hour of life and light,
To serve and lift with all that genius brings;
Then slip into the darkness shrouding sight;
Are swift forgotten, while Time ceaseless
      wings:
   Yet that which deeply stirs another soul
   Will last through all the aeons' endless roll.

So sweet St. Francis, wandering through the
      fields
And olive groves of sunny Italy;
Teaching the joy the life of spirit yields,
Striving to help the blind of soul to see,
Knowing the power the poor in spirit wields,
Loving the world of bird and flower and tree:
   Is not his life a symbol, now as then,
   Of all that will redeem the world of men?

Men need today, as every yesterday,
To be called back from senseless rush for gold,
And fashion, dissipation—all the way

That dulls the heart of life and makes it cold—
Back to love, work and simple, joyous play
Of those emotions that can ne'er grow old:
    'T is not a gospel new that mankind needs;
    But the old gospel born in loving deeds.

[Dresden, Germany, July 13, 1907]

THE *Sistine Madonna* bears study again and again. I had thought I remembered it just as it was; but now it comes upon me with a new revelation. It is one of the few works of art in the world of which one may say, "it is absolutely satisfying," that is, it accomplishes perfectly what the artist intended. Raphael has never deeply drawn me—appreciation of him has been with the head rather than the heart. His regular grace, ease of execution and smooth serenity have left me cold; in contrast to the appeal of depth and struggle in Michael Angelo, of masterly power and humanity in Leonardo da Vinci, of the personal tenderness and unavailing reach of Andrea del Sarto. Raphael usually satisfies my imagination, without stimulating and arousing as the others do; but to the sweeping power of this painting one confesses unqualified response. It expresses, adequately and harmoniously, the highest spiritual aspiration and mysticism of mediæval religious life. Raphael has taken the human maiden and mother, pure, tender, graceful, beautiful, and lifted her to the skies.

85

What a reach of wonder in the deep, far-looking, yet tenderly human eyes. She looks down, across what one may suppose to be the awed and kneeling multitude, toward which San Sisto points, touched, it is true, with the pathos of life, but dominated by a tender, exultant awe in the vision of the spiritual meaning of it all. The same vision, less softened and warmed with the human, is in the eyes of the Christ-child. The sense of it is given in the myriad angel faces composing the blue atmosphere of the background. The simply human mood is in the tender smile of Santa Barbara; while the prayer for grace fills the face of San Sisto. The dear, light feet of the Madonna scarcely touch the clouds—so full of airy grace she seems.

Is it not puzzling that in no other work of Raphael's is there a hint that this conception and power were in his soul? Strange, that he should have done this once only; and that, wanting this achievement, the world could not have guessed this possibility was within him. Does this result from the fact that he was the finished artist, doing easily and perfectly what he conceived—not the dreamer of vast dreams.

beyond human power of execution, nor the struggling aspirant, attempting deeps of thought no painting can embody, but which, even haltingly expressed, challenge the imagination beyond the harmonious perfection of finished art?

Four Faces

FOUR masters of the unrivalled Renaissance:
Each his own portrait painting for the world—
A self-confession of the soul of life,
The high desires, the tragedies and dreams.

Serene and placid, the unfurrowed face:
High aspiration and the joy of youth,
A chastened eagerness, with keen response
To popes and princes, patrons of his art:
The face of one achieving easily,
With graceful beauty, each inspiring dream:
No tragic lines that tell of struggles deep
To image what transcends all forms of art;
Eternal youth, with calm of conscious power:
The face of Raphael.

Like to an age-old pine upon the slope
Of ragged and rocky mountains, seamed and
        scarred
By centuries of battle with the storms:
Such is the face of Michael Angelo.

Deep furrows of thought and pain across the
      brow;
The lips compressed with constant self-con-
      trol;
Eyes that look out and away to visions wide,
That reach beyond our sphere to heights sub-
      lime;
Unanswered hunger, telling the desire
For warm appreciation from mankind,
That should respond to writhing Titan forms
Embodying the fragments of his dream;
Yet power to rise above the world of men
And do the great work, lonely and apart:
Such is the tragic, time-scarred face of him
Who wrought the forms for Medicean tombs
And on the Sistine ceiling painted all
The history and destiny of man.

    Lofty and self-contained, with calm clear
      brow,
Beneath the locks of long and graying hair;
Upon the lips a touch of cynic scorn,
From age-long gaze across the vanity
Of human life: a face serene and strong,
With virile mastery and conscious power,
Of one who towered above his fellows, like

FOUR FACES

Some Himalayan peak that rises far
To still communion with the winds and stars:
Such is the face of Leonardo, he
Who greatness won in every field of art
And intellect; whose ruined masterpiece
Amazes on the Milan convent wall—
The solemn supper of Jesus and the twelve.

Tender and wan, with hunger of the heart,
For answer that never came to lift through love
To heights of joy and power to clothe in form
The high ideal that brooded in his soul:
Painted in light and shadow, and sensitive;
The tender lips with sad compression shut;
The longing eyes, sad brow and tangled hair:
The face of one who might have risen to heights
Unequalled, had love lifted him; but who,
With love misplaced, could be led on and on,
Till, tangled in the web of life, he found
Ambition dead and the ideal gone:
Andrea del Sarto.

Four masters of the unrivalled Renaissance:
Their portraits framed upon Italian walls:
Four who achieved the heights above the
        throng;

Yet *men:* each life unique, vibrant, intense
With our humanity, containing all
The mystery within the heart of man.

RAPHAEL AND ANGELO

[Rome, August, 1907]

ANGELO was the giant, Raphael the painter of beautiful forms. One was brooded over by vast dreams and conceptions, the other stimulated by applause and popular favor, acting on a native genius. The one is doomed almost inevitably to tragedy; while the other is immediately and brilliantly successful.

What a Rome—that contained two such men at the same time, with a Julius II to spur them on!

Raphael and Angelo—it is the eternal struggle: should art produce beautiful forms, or should it reveal the content of the human spirit and teach the meaning of life? Should it be beautiful or significant? It must be both: ah, yes, but it is difficult indeed to bring the two elements into balanced union, as in a Shakespeare; and so the eternal struggle goes on. As it has been said that all minds are temperamentally Platonic or Aristotelian, aspiring toward the cause—God, or seeking to understand the effect—the world, so all minds are instinctively admirers of Raphael or Angelo—naturally responding to the satisfying appeal of grace and beauty, or drawn to the profound

struggle to embody dreams and ideals that out-
reach the forms of art.   Tennyson and Brown-
ing, Mozart and Beethoven, Sophocles and
Aeschylus—the same contrast and struggle run
through all art, as in life, too, though there the
elements are more confusedly mingled.

Giordano Bruno

[In his cell the night before his execution: Rome, February 16, 1600. Through the barred window a glimpse of the heaven of stars.]

SO to its end the long way draws at last!
   My feet that wearily have travelled all
The stony path beset with thorns shall now
Find rest at last.   At last this beating heart
That hungered so to bless, redeem mankind—
A half-hour's flaming agony, and then
The peace!
   Peace silencing the mob's exultant cry
Of joy to see a heretic in flames.
And I—the living, breathing, thirsting man,
I whose strong vision reached beyond the stars
And knew the God of infinite majesty,
Creator of all rolling suns that burn
Their way through space with swift attendant
         worlds,
Inhabited like ours with thinking minds,
Akin to God and knowing him as sons—
Shall *I* be gone?   My body dissipated
In air; my soul a breath—no more?
Ah God, if this were so, how could I bear

94

The flames' hot horror!   But no!   E'en then
      I should
Accept the fate, dreaming that through my
      death
The world I gave my life for might go on
To know a freedom in some far-off time,
Unlike the brutal chains and gloomy cells
Men give today to those who save the world.
    And she—Lucia—girl who loved me well
At Naples and again at Venice, when
Fate beckoned me across the Alps, and I,
Hungering for my country, heard the call
And came to find the doom I dreaded there!
Then eight long years slow moving hour by
      hour,
In silence underneath the convent's walls,
With just this little gleam of stars to lift
My soul from blank despair.   No book or pen,
No page to take the wealth of garnered thought
I yearn to give a world that sleeps in chains!
    O stars that shine beyond my window's bars
Shall I ascend to you when through the flames'
Hot malice all my body's pain is gone?
    Lucia, what of you?   Ah! did they dare
To blot you out of life when I was chained?
O God!   the agony to wither here

While you were starving for one healing kiss!
But now 'tis o'er: tomorrow morn the end—
Like healing balm the fire will scorch my limbs,
And, rising quickly to my heart and face,
Release me from this living death entombed.
    I die a martyr—Yes, as true as saints
Who heard God call them from the sky above
And saw the jewelled crown awaiting there.
Yet dare I claim such name who stand alone,
Outcast by all whose lives I sought to lift
With light of truth and call to liberty?
Dishonored, outlaw, loved of none, I stand
A martyr for the light of intellect—
God's mind that sends illuminating rays
To minds of men, too blind to know their lot.
My day will dawn: across the misty years,
I see arise a race untrammelled, free,
Open to Nature's every secret law,
Erect and fearless in the face of all
The midnight gloom that threatens from the
        past.
O brothers ye will know me at the last,
And Bruno's name will shine among the few
To which men bow as prophets of the dawn!
    Then come the flame!—God's light become
        a fire

To doom instead of bless, since human hands
Misuse their power and curse His gifts with
    shame.
Shine on, ye suns that burn your trackless way
Through reaches vast of space toward some dim
    goal!
The soul of man is vaster far than ye
And dares to meet the world on equal terms.
My soul shall live, swept out into the void,
And I shall know the meaning of it all!
    Alone, unfriended, murdered by your hands,
I love you, O my brothers, and my thought
Shall flow a rivulet across the years
Till, gathering from the mountains climbed by
    those
God sends to strike his water from the rock,
The river deep and broad shall sweep the fields
And carry living water to the souls
Who dare to drink from intellect's calm stream.
Let come the flames! A martyr willingly
I die that ye may live and truth may dawn!

THE ENGLISH CEMETERY

[Rome, Italy, August 5, 1907]

NO other cemetery is so moving as the little English burying ground near the Pyramid of Cestius. How many exiles sleep there—far from home! How many artists' hopes—all unfulfilled—lie buried there! How many names written, not even in water, in the world's larger life, fade from the mouldering stones! The trees whisper over them, while beside them, the busy, careless modern city surges on, with the countless lives that soon will be gone. The hungry-faced, beautiful children beg in the alleys; the dissipated men and pandering women drink in the cafés; the ambitious boys cry their petty wares to the crowds of curious travellers; while silently apart, in Colosseum, Forum, on the Palatine Hill and in the ever appearing walls and arches, brood the significant memories of two thousand years. Ah, human life—how carelessly, unthinkingly, each generation lives its hot, brief span and adds itself to the speaking silence of the all-overarching past!

Italy Called

I SEEMED to hear a far-off call,
  I longed that you should go with me
Across the sea's enclosing wall
To dwell in sun-kissed Italy.

But now I know my wish was vain,
For what is any land to me,
And what care I for sun or rain,
Since in your heart is Italy.

There is one only call I hear—
'Tis not the call to wander wide;
The only call that moves me, Dear,
Is just to be where you abide.

I long no more o'er seas to roam,
I ask not far-off lands to see—
Where you are, Darling, is my home,
In your heart, Love, my Italy.

'Tis not the sun that shines above
That fills my heart and soul with light,

But the full sunshine of your love
That sweeps away my inner night.

Could I but fly to you, dear Heart,
And in your eyes the love-light see,
To be with you and never part—
Then would I have my Italy!

[Vredeoord, July 5, 1914]

TO the man of thought, already cosmopolitan, the chief value of travel is in tremendously stimulating the flow of ideas and in contributing a wealth of illustrations. One may travel also through books and reflections. If the stimulation is less acute than that through the outer senses, it is wider in range and more fully at one's command, without the waste and strain of movement from place to place. There are advantages to the stay-at-home, as well as for the traveller. If one opportunity is denied, use the other more sacredly.

Marcus Aurelius

[Standing at a window of his palace, looking out over the sleeping imperial city of Rome, 178, A. D.]

FOR forty years the burden I have borne—
   The weight of this vast empire that I
   rule—
Rule?   *Serve,* far more a slave than meanest
   one
Of all my subjects in this world-wide realm.
How many thousand days and nights of toil
I have spent on legal cases, brought to me,
The ultimate law-maker of the world.
I sought to mete out justice, and still more
To humanize the stubborn code of law,
That clings to precedent, and so hands on
The old barbarities from age to age.
   As though this endless toil were not enough
Recurring came the call to meet the storm
Of wild barbaric tribes, who ceaseless knock
Upon the empire's doors, with growing threat
To overwhelm Rome's never-conquered might.
Seven unbroken years I ruled my realm

From soldier's tent on changing battle fields;
My capital not seen in all those years—
My capital that hourly grows in vice,
In mere licentiousness and cruel lust.
　I gaze o'er stately palaces to where
Moon-lit the mighty Colosseum stands,
A monument to Roman power, still more
A monument to Roman lust for blood.
The gladiators that I took with me,
Once only, that their fight might be for Rome,
And not to make a Roman holiday,
Fought well; yet how the people murmured
　　　loud,
And even threatened me, since they had lost
The sport that gave its zest to life—Ah me!
What mean the Gods?　Their High Priest in
　　　the state,
I ever sought to mould the minds of men
To reverent worship and obedience;
Yet swift Rome reels to ruin.　Ever more
The ominous knocking at her weakened doors;
While here, degraded men, licentious women
Flaunt their bold vices to the templed Gods.
　And he, Commodus, is he then my son?
Rapacious, lustful, cruel, what a fate
Awaits for Rome and for the world, should he

Become sole monarch of this darkening realm!
Faustina, daughter of one revered and loved,
The pious Antoninus, mother of him
They call my son, what evil power inspired
Your heart and gave your lawless wild de-
    sires!
    The Gods are just and wise, and what they
      will
We may not understand, but must accept.
To you, O Universe, I bow my head:
Nothing is early or late that pleases you;
And since the poet, "City of Cecrops" said,
May we not also say, Dear City of God?
For opening scene the signal came of God;
And He gives sign for silent curtain fall:
Nor one nor other changes at our will;
We can but bow and say, His will be done!
    The ruin coming I could not avert,
Only postpone—the lurid sunset hour
Of Roman grandeur. Swift the night will
    come,
A night chaotic, black with ruin vast.
    The day is gone; beneath the silent stars,
I wrap my Roman cloak about me close;
And with a sigh that mingles glad relief
And bitter pain, lie down to sleep at last!

[Glen Hill Farm, Twin Mountain, N. H., August 11, 1909]

THE changing beauty of these mountains! All day yesterday the clouds gathered and drew away: now sending a down-pour of rain that shut one in; and now lifting to reveal a sea of blue ranges, clear and clean in color, rising to a deep band of pearl sky; while to the left the scurrying gray clouds lent deeper gloom to the dark pine-covered slopes of the nearer giants.

Today the air is cold, the sun radiant, with just clouds enough to give an ever-changing play of light and shadow. How calm and beautiful it all is; and in what contrast to the fevered haste and confusion of the human life in the cities!

"Autumn In Everything"

[Sapphic stanzas]

THE gold of the autumn woods is dull and
    sombre,
Touched with the gray of the leaden clouds
    that lower,
Turning even the red to a gloomy mantle,
    Dark and forbidding.

Even as the autumn day is my heart that sor-
    rows,
Filled with the pain of death and of fruitless
    longing,
Reaching through the mist of the tears that
    blind me
      To find but the shadow!

[Montclair, N. J., June 13, 1909]

THOREAU is like a breath of out-doors— an excursion into the Nature-world; yet all his writings show clearly the limitations of the man. Accurate observation at times passes over into triviality; self-sufficiency may become conceit; emphasis of the common descends at times to contentment with the commonplace. Thoreau's reaction is healthy and corrective; but extreme and one-sided. There is a certain barrenness in his voluntarily limited life. Sincere living to oneself gives earnest dignity; but the absence of stimulation from the great human world makes it easy to pass over into the puerile. The oriental mystic, at his best, is absorbed in the contemplation of Brahma; at his worst, he spends much time looking at his navel.

Thoreau *lived* Emerson's *Self-Reliance* and *Heroism,* and perhaps furnished a theme for Emerson's thinking; but his *Journals* needed just the sifting Emerson gave to his own work in the finished *Essays.* The limitations of Thoreau's thinking are particularly evident in his judgment of such a widely experienced worldling as Goethe, where he becomes childishly amateurish.

The emphasis, nevertheless, is tonic and challenging. Thoreau's hold on simple reality, opposition to the worship of possessions, immediate response to the beauty and truth of Nature, with a somewhat wide appreciation of great literature, make him even more corrective to the glaring faults of our time, than to those of the period for which he wrote. Equally is this true of his manly protest against, not only convention and conformity, but misguided philanthropy and meddlesome reform. There are even more fanatics to be rebuked now than then.

Thoreau illustrates, too, how an advancing age develops a common atmosphere, influencing all the men of the time. Passage after passage reads like a more whimsical Emerson; but with no evidence of imitation. The affirmative method of expression, the emphasis of the spirit rather than the things that serve it, the self-sufficiency, the philosophic yet . romantic response to Nature, the ethical optimism: these all belong to Transcendentalism in New England.

[Twin Mountain, N. H., August 19, 1911]

NATURE is beautiful in every mood, if one accepts her changes without irritation. This gray storm, with dark, lowering sky, white wisps of detached clouds floating against the nearer hills, occasional showers of rain, an irregular wind that rises at quick intervals to brush the balsam boughs against the windows and waken the grove of them to music: all this, with the foreground of the solitary study and the fire of logs upon the hearth, is inexpressibly beautiful, if one will but accept responsively the mood of the day.

Gethsemane

INTO that lone valley, dim and low,
  You came and placed your woman's hand
    in mine;
Leading me forth to where God's summits shine,
And lifting from my heart its weight of woe.
Ah Dear, how could you drop my hand and go
There, whence my anguished struggles bring
      no sign?
Again in rayless dark my heart must pine,
Bowed down beneath the unexpected blow.

Ah, how for me you poured, in days gone by,
The wine of love from your o'er-flowing heart:
So quick to answer every hungry cry,
And tenderly to heal each slightest smart;
And now in bitter loneliness I lie,
And weep the Fate that holds us wide apart!

[Glen Hill Farm, July 27, 1906]

HOW impossible to describe the beauty of these mountains—a beauty soft, genial, tender, yet infinite in variety, changing with each hour of the day and each day of the year. Before, rises the green slope of Beech Hill; while to the right is fold on fold of mountains, blue, soft, mysterious, played upon by ever-changing shadows, deepening in color as evening comes, suggesting an infinite reach of beauty and mystery. To the left, appear rugged, bold outlines, deeper tones and more towering forms. Behind, are densely-wooded slopes, dark green color, shadows ever moving—a background for the peaceful meadowlands just below.

What ever-inspiring beauty, to rest, invigorate, give new power to mind and body! Ah! the soul has gone out of it all. The beauty that should heal and inspire, brings tears to the eyes; yet the world goes on: the liquid note of the Hermit Thrush echoes from the trees; the sun declines and the shadows soften; light deepens on the distant hills: the night will come!

FROM THE STUDY

[Glen Hill Farm, August 22, 1911]

THIS northern Nature world is prolific, if not luxuriant. What a wealth of delicate mosses, each with its own peculiar growth and beauty. The innumerable grasses and ferns, lovely flowering plants, and above all, the marvelous growth of the trees, from the myriad shoots starting up from the sod to the splendid annual increase of the balsams and the pines: all unite in an expression of wondrously fertile life.

How simple and healthful are the pleasures of the Nature world in contrast to those of the city. The wind music is ever singing. The birch trees across from my open doors yield a fluttering, rustling, aspen-like melody; while the evergreens sigh and whisper far more deeply of the mystery of things. Then the play of light and shadow: the birches quiver with changing light, one great spruce broods over its black shadow, while the tall ripened grasses bend and wave in a golden wonder of beauty. Over all is the blue of the sky and the sunshine of this radiant day. How much saner and sweeter it all is than the salacious vaudeville of the thronged theatres and the over-laden tables of the garish restaurants of the city.

Alone

WILDLY the night-winds moan,
   The clouds blow darkly o'er,
I am alone, alone,
Alone for evermore!

Yon pine cries ghostly shrill,
I shudder as a child;
I have nor thought nor will,
My heart beats vainly wild.

The storm-winds howl and moan,
The clouds blow darkly o'er,
I am alone, alone,
Alone for evermore!

[Glen Hill Farm, September 12, 1909]

A MARVELOUS Sunday morning—my last day here for this year. The morning clouds have drawn away; the sun is radiant but soft; the air is cool, if one gets into the shadow; a light breeze, at intervals, stirs the trees; while the mountains are entrancing in soft blue beauty, rising range beyond range. The shadows are deep beneath the larger trees; the play of soft color, tinged with autumn, transfigures the rolling meadows, and the mood is one of peace and dreams.

The Call Of Arcady

O FAIR sweet wind of Arcady,
I hear thy summons woodlands o'er;
I hear thy whisper at the door,
O fair sweet wind of Arcady.

A bird song echoes from the tree,
The shadows tremble on the floor,
The children's voices softly soar
From out the garden glades to me.

I will arise and answer thee,
Thy call is echoed more and more,
From meadow sweet and pine tree hoar,
Thou fair sweet wind of Arcady.

O that my weary eyes could see
The sight they long have hungered for—
Some Greek nymph beckon from the door
To forest dell as fair as she.

Then would my youth return to me,
My heart that now is troubled sore,

Would learn from her dear kisses' lore,
The secret of what love may be.

The nymphs are gone; and from the sea
No Aphrodite rises more:
Ah, cease your whisper at the door,
Sad lying wind of Arcady!

[August 11, 1911]

THE laws of art and the laws of nature are related, but not the same. Just as the artist, to interpret character, must discover and portray the one, out of the myriad actual or possible expressions, that best reveals the personality, so he must find and choose, out of the thousand shapes the drapery may take in Nature, the one most beautiful and portray that. That is, lines, forms and colors must not only be true to Nature, they must conform also to the need of the human senses and intellect. That is why the mere transcript from reality is at times so wonderful, at other times, so offensive.

PIERRE LOUŸS

[Vredeoord, September 15, 1910]

THE stories of Pierre Louÿs are masterly
work, with marvelous delicacy of style,
limpid beauty and gripping power; yet reveal-
ing, withal, a spirit of non-moral beauty-
worship, verging on the perverse. Must it be
so? Cannot the Venus-worship coexist with
clean wholesomeness and strong, sweet life?
Must it ever turn to unhealthy sex-desire and
morbid blood-lust?

Though these stories are as perfect in sen-
suous simplicity as the prose poems of the Eng-
lish contemporary of Louÿs, Oscar Wilde, there
is in them, with even stronger sex and beauty
worship, the same impression of decadence, of
refinement pushed to the point of morbidity.
Is it that the beauty worshipped is *all* of the
body, with no sacred expression of the soul?
The charm is compelling; yet one draws back.
This is the modern *Venusberg,* drawing no vi-
rile Tannhäuser to a strong sensual riot; but
subtly entrapping the over-refined artist, whose
worn nerves ache with sensuous desire, to a
debauch of the imagination, of which the only
physical expression is in perverted action, and

which is without any vision of the true spirit of man and woman.

Still, the words seem too strong, and the mysterious fascination remains; while the true Venus-worship stands as a sound reaction upon that other perversion—ascetic revolt against the flesh and its beauty and truth. How shall the true religion be attained, that avoids both perversions and walks the straight path between, loving and enjoying all the beauty of the body, but always as the enrobing garment of the spirit behind?

The Hope Of Spring

WHEN the earth draws nearer and nearer
    the sun,
She laughs out her joy in grass and flowers;
The ice-brooks melt and the waters run
Through the forest—all fragrant bowers.

When I draw nearer and nearer to you,
O wondrous, joy-giving sun of my heart,
My death-chilled soul is born anew,
While, for flowers, the warm tears start.

[Canyon, Texas, July 10, 1921]

THE Red River Canyon is without the stupendous grandeur of the Grand Canyon; but it has a beauty and sublimity of its own. Appearing suddenly in the vast, sweeping plain, its broad chasm, flanked by shelving terraces, sheers down to a great depth. The many-colored strata of its irregular walls, red, yellow and lavender, give barbaric magnificence, especially when the morning or evening light plays magic with the colors and softens the savage rock masses with a mist of rays of light. Here and there red pyramids rise, like Aztec temples to forgotten gods.

A thin stream drops down a dizzy fall, and behind it, on the vast, rounded wall, swallows build their clay nests. Here and there are scattering, old, wind-torn cedars, while the nearer floor of the Canyon is carpeted with a mass of purple flowers. Majestically impressive and rebukingly beautiful it is.

The Plains

[The West Texas Panhandle, July 8, 1921]

WIDE circle of plains stretching away,
 The rim rising up to touch the sky;
Illusory mountains, majestic and white,
Formed on the circle's rim,
By great masses of changing clouds;
Intense light pouring down from the sun,
On the green and brown flat land.
Gathering clouds, and the passing threat of a
  storm;
The massed clouds breaking and drawing away;
The sunset glory turning them
To a wonder of red and gold.
An hour of twilight, and the rush of chill even-
  ing air;
The night and a cloudless dome of sky,
Filled with a marvel of brilliant shining stars:
Such is the changing day and its beauty,
In the great, wide sweep of the high and lim-
  itless plains.

[June 26, 1919]

THE world has been living too fast ever since the industrial revolution in modern society; and this is particularly true of America. Everywhere is the feverish haste. The leisurely production of great art has practically disappeared. At best we have studies, experiments; at worst, stuff hastily produced to meet some surface whim of popular taste. It is the attitude toward life that is fundamentally wrong—the ceaseless struggle to get, instead of to give and grow.

Somehow, education must awaken a love and appreciation of the real things of life, instead of the adventitious, and cultivate the wise use of leisure. This is the education for life, that must balance that for vocation and efficiency.

[On Train, January 31, 1919]

OKLAHOMA and Texas represent an emulsion of the West and the South, with the traditions of the South still dominant. When the emulsion becomes a solution, the sectionalism of that part of the country will be gone.

Something of old Southern hospitality, a strong infusion of Western energy, the forward look and gambling spirit of the frontier: these compose the vigorous, coarse life that pulsates here.

Gray Is The Sky

GRAY is the sky and misty gray are the
mountains,
The trees darkened down to the sombre mood
of tears;
Gray is the mood of the heart and brackish its
fountains,
The dumb dull ache annulling all hopes and
fears.

Winds may come and sweep the boughs of the
forest,
Clearing the sky and sounding the melody
deep:
Wanting the love to cleanse the heart that is
sorest,
What cures but the silence—the silence of end-
less sleep!

REPOSE IN THE SPIRIT

[Vredeoord, July, 1914]

REPOSE of spirit has all but gone from this modern life—at least in cities. Repose is, however, a spiritual fact, not one of place and outer condition. Napoleon had repose in the midst of a battle, and Lincoln in a crowd. Withdraw into the solitude of the spirit to dominate distracting things.

Do not allow yourself to be pulled out of your own sphere. Go on living with the great masters. The eternal things will outlive the interests on the surface: trust to them and wait.

It is foolish to be ever postponing life and existing in anticipation of what is just ahead. Wherever one is and under whatever circumstances, one should seek to live each moment to the full. If every other phase of opportunity seems cut off, one can at least garner wisdom.

[St. Louis, Mo., June 21, 1919]

HOW purely conventional the forms of modesty are: they seem to have little to do with its essential spirit. This is particularly evident in the dress of women. Display, that five years ago would have attracted salacious attention and comment, today passes quite unnoticed. It is only the first unveiling that excites: the moment it is a custom, it ceases to arouse unusual response. Since beauty adds greatly to the joy of life, in general the more it is revealed by the dress of women, the better, provided the display is a customary habit.

This is what the zealots and philistine reformers fail to understand, as with the nude in art.

Sunday In The City

[Kansas City, Mo., January 9, 1921]

FAINT winter sunlight weakly oozing
    down,
Girls with rouged cheeks, short skirts and
    bizarre stockings,
Legs, legs, legs,—displayed like a green-gro-
    cer's carrots
To tempt languid passers-by;
Strolling families pausing to look at the
    marked-down goods in the shops,
Glare of bill-boards before moving-picture
    houses,
Strident clang of street-car gongs,
Harsh-throated cars before which people scud
Like autumn leaves raised by a sudden gust—
    Sunday in the City!

[Chautauqua, N. Y., August 11, 1914]

IT seems strange to be working quietly here, while the greatest cataclysm in the history of the world is on in Europe. What will come out of it all: a realignment of nations; changed relations of the United States with the rest of the world; perhaps the end of autocracy in Europe: who can guess? The situation and its possible consequences simply stagger the imagination.

[Vredeoord, September 10, 1914]

HOW private griefs and hardships shrink in significance in the presence of this terrible War! Democracy is on trial as never before. With the transformation of modern armament, can free men repeat the tradition of Marathon and Salamis? Can they fight better than the soulless machine of the autocrat; and so protect themselves against tyranny and military beaurocracy? If not, then democracy is doomed; if they can, then democracy will be immeasurably strengthened throughout the world.

It will be better if the War is not a drawn

battle, but a fight to the clear settlement of the issues involved.

[Vredeoord September 20, 1914]

THERE are many factors in this War— race hatreds, national selfishness, economic jealousies—but at bottom it is a struggle between democracy and military despotism. The hope is that when the Germans themselves come to see this, they will make an end of such despotism, in Germany at least.

[Vredeoord, May 29, 1915]

HOW this terrible fact of War falls across all our philosophies. Complacent optimisms are put out of court by it. The pleasant interpretations mediocrity formulates of the universe are torn to tatters. There is at least the refreshment of standing face to face with brute actuality, though it crash all our "little systems" to the ground. Philosophy must wait: the interpretation cannot be hastened, while the facts are multiplying with such confusing celerity. The one certainty is that an entirely new era will be ushered in: what it will be, no one knows.

[Vredeoord, May 31, 1915]

THE first radiant summer day, after weeks of rain and gloom. Nature goes quietly on, just as if the world were not aflame with devastating war. One needs to look across the hideous present. As Nature quickly covers over the worst scars we make in her calm and all-fecund breast, so man has a power of recovery, after great strain and tragic suffering, beyond all we could have dreamed. It is to that one must look, across this time of demonic destruction.

[Vredeoord, June 4, 1915]

STRANGE! that personal joys and sorrows still loom large, in the face of this world tragedy. One is ashamed to feel them so deeply; yet so it must always be. The little world is the soul of the larger world; and it is only what we feel in personal life that interprets to us the colossal tragedies of mankind.

Heart O' Mine

HEART of mine, Alas! the precious days
    are passing,
Drearily the distance stretches out between!
Were you with me I could banish cares
    harassing,
All forget the troubled hours I have seen.

Dear, I worship all the wonder of your spirit—
Keenest humor, quick response and joy in life,
Voice that plays upon my heart-strings when
    I hear it,
Eyes that glow with love that lifts me o'er
    the strife.

What a dower of wondrous beauty you inherit!
Youth that is eternal dwells in your dear
    heart.
Would I might do all that you so richly
    merit—
Lift you, free from care, into a heaven apart!

All I am I give you, yours to keep forever,
You are life and all beneath heaven's dome;
I must wander far and wide: O may I ever
Find the path that takes me to your heart—
       my home!

[New York City, July 15, 1911]

RODIN'S *Hand of God* is, to me, the most impressive of his works in the Metropolitan. The daring conception is adequately carried out. Delicately moulded, the gigantic hand seems to sink into the stone. In the palm, swirl together the two human figures, absorbed in their own love, but grasped firmly and yet tenderly in the hand that is at once Fate and Father. Life, Destiny, Mystery—the Transient and the Eternal: all are here!

DOES Rodin's struggle for significance make him almost bizarre? Consider the *Hand of God* or even *The Thinker*: one gets the idea in each, but it is almost forced, lacking the sense of tremendous reserve power that is in all the work of Michael Angelo. Still, it is indeed refreshing to find a master who has great ideas, who always *means something*, in a time of such technical fooling and display as prevail today.

Unity

THERE is one spirit whispers in the flow-
    ers,
One thought repeated everywhere we turn;
Each thing we see contains the whole of Na-
    ture,
Of man and God, within its humble being,
And strives as far as is within its power
To realize the Eternal Spirit still.

As harp within the skillful master's hand
Gives forth the music sweet that charms the
    soul,
As light upon the evening clouds doth paint
Visions of the vast silence to inspire
With awe and infinite longing the full hearts
With which men gaze upon the heavenly sight,
So may I be within the hand of Him
Who is the whole which we divided see.

[On Train, October 31, 1917]

TRUE sacrifice is unknown to the present generation of Americans. Many have experienced suffering through disease, poverty, the death of loved ones; but this private tragedy has been accepted as natural misfortune; while voluntary sacrifice—the giving up of pleasure, comfort, ease, money, time, life, for the sake of a great cause—has not been demanded of the people as a whole since the Civil War. Thus the supreme call of the present tragic hour is entirely new to this generation.

What will it do to us? Surely it must awaken a new serious view of life. We shall be forced to think in terms of something larger than ourselves and our own ease and comfort. At least, this must come, if we accept the call and rise to the sacrifice heroically.

THE adaptability of human nature is one of its most wonderful characteristics. The way our minds accept the world tragedy is as surprising as our soldiers' adjustment to the privations, miseries and dangers of the actual conflict. Sufferings that would have seemed impossible to bear, come to be taken for granted. I suppose it is this quality that explains how the race has survived through so many disasters and continued to go forward.

[November 9, 1917]

VOLUNTARY cooperation is what American democracy has been slow to learn; but suffering and sacrifice are drastic teachers, forcing people to make common cause. Already, we are beginning to learn the lesson. Everywhere, in conversation and print, people are substituting "we" for "I". So we may waken to find the old rampant individualism gone, without our knowing it; and a new social instinct of cooperation strongly in its place.

[Greeley, Colo., July 30, 1918]

PEOPLE have become a little dulled to the horror of the War. Now they are thrilled with the glory of American achievement. Day by day, the horrible destruction goes on. Four full years, and the end is not in sight yet!

How utterly the War changes the destiny of individuals: because a youth was born in a certain decade, he must give up, for a period of years, the direction of his own life, leave family and friends, face possible mutilation or death, and if he returns, find his future entirely changed.

Colorado is further from the War in spirit than any other place I have been. It is hard to realize that there is a war, with this radiant sunshine, blossoming earth and prosperous people. It will take the direct personal losses to bring the War home here.

HOW long will it be till the world learns to stop utterly the stupid and blindly wasteful solution, war is for human quarrels? Not, I suppose, until the last irresponsible autocrats and castes are overthrown. Nor does this mean the substitution of the tyranny of the largest for the smallest class. The Bolshevists are just as irresponsibly despotic as were the czar and the aristocracy.

Neither would the substitution of cut-throat economic warfare be the solution. Until friendly international cooperation is achieved, under the rule of established and accepted law, the shadow of war will ever threaten on the horizon. One generation learns tragically the frightful lesson, but the next forgets and must often learn it anew. If only, under the multiplied horror of the lesson this time, mankind can definitely apply it in action and work toward the solution!

The Cost

[January 28, 1919]

THE War is ended, the fighting done,
  With joy all free hearts leap;
The troops are coming, with honors won—
But what of the boys who sleep?

We turn to the tasks of peace once more,
We sow and the harvest reap;
The children play by the cottage door—
But what of the boys who sleep?

O life is sweet and good, forsooth,
With its loves and longings deep;
It is sad to die in the flush of youth,
Like the dear, brave lads who sleep.

Alone they sit in the silence lost,
With hearts too full to weep—
Mothers and wives who have paid the cost—
And dream of the boys who sleep!

[Chicago, December 15, 1918]

STRANGE to live through months in which history is making with a swiftness and reach unequalled in the entire past! I suppose, because people are so close to the gigantic sweep of events, they do not see it. A little later, and men will be awe-struck at what has happened. Still, the world takes the greatest changes for granted, once they are accomplished; and goes on, unthinkingly, with its routine of work and play.

What people need is to be disturbed in their complacency. The heroic possibility is in every one: it is the routine and inertia that chain it down. The War has proved that.

Leisure of the spirit: that is what America lacks. She has energy, faith, idealism, but she does not see thoughtfully nor live quietly and beautifully. "Life's fitful fever" is her story —unrecognized. With recognition should come the cure.

The Cup Of The Darker Drink

[To W. C. B., June, 1914]

THE angel at the pathway's brink,
  With saddened face, reluctant stands;
The bitter cup within his hands
He proffers, bidding you to drink.

The time has come to sift the past
And find the meaning of the days,
Using the sun's last fading rays
To garner wisdom that will last.

The petty answers, little minds
Contrive for all the joy and pain,
Conceal beneath a dogma vain
The mysteries the spirit finds.

We know alone the little arc—
God's circled truth is all too great,
Our poor philosophy must wait—
And yet the circle's curve we mark;

And dare to trust it rounds the whole,
That life will be, as life has been,

That all the garnered fruit we glean
Will live forever in the soul.

The resignation of the weak
Is idle: easy is the end
For those who to their sorrows bend
And, wearied, know no more to seek.

While he who longs to meet the day
And feels achievement but begun,
Must weep to know his day is done
And, grieving, take the lonely way.

Yet though the body weaken fast,
With will serene the soul may rise,
A stoic calm within the eyes
That face the future as the past.

The shadows deepen to the night:
Courageous, take the cup of woe,
Drink to the bitter dregs, and know:
Beyond the shadows is the light!

MORALE AND MILITARISM

[St. Louis, Mo., June 21, 1919]

WITH high morale, it is possible swiftly to acquire training; but long-continued discipline will not create morale. The victory of America has destroyed the superstition that the longest and most thorough training will make an army invincible. Courage, tenacity, unconquerable heroism depend upon the soul—upon caring for something so high, that life is not to be considered in comparison. It is because we had that spirit that our troops, with a few months' training, were able to break the German armies, with their forty years of discipline, and win the War. Incidentally, we broke the tradition of professional militarism forever, and freed democracy from the superstition that it must be accepted for secure defense.

OUR returning soldier young men have all the same attitude: glad and proud to have fought for the great cause, but hoping never to have anything to do with military life again. With this feeling dominant among our soldiers, in spite of our swift and brilliant victories, there is little danger of professional militarism here. As a people we resent war and all that pertains and leads to it; but if we are challenged and forced to fight, we fight, as we do everything else, with all the energy and strength we possess.

AFTER THE WAR

[State College, Pa., July 20, 1920]

HOW quickly youth recovers: the War is forgotten, the young men who died are rarely remembered, youth laughs and goes on. *Youth never looks backward.* Doubtless it is life's way with us. Already the War is but an interesting past adventure—to all but the mutilated and the old people who mourn. Tagore says, "Europe is dancing on her coffin." Well, when one considers the innumerable multitude of the dead, perhaps it is well that they can dance!

The nation is tired with the long strain of high thinking and feeling compelled by the War: hence the present inertia and reaction. People do not want to think nor feel too deeply. There is a widespread desire for distraction and titillation, an unwillingness to work hard.

The same attitude prevails toward wise economy: thrift takes thought. The view seems to be: since costs are so high, why try to save; buy what you can, and stop thinking about it. There could be no more impressive evidence of the predominance of psychological over economic factors in the movement of human society.

A sickness of spirit is abroad. Life seems not to present its normal ends. One wonders toward what the youth of this generation aspire. We seem to be living in an interim between significant movements. A difficult epoch; and yet, as always, life is made of the great, simple realities of the spirit, and somehow human beings will find and live them.

Lincoln

[Boston, February 12, 1921]

LINCOLN, thou art our great American:
  Guiding through war-swept seas the ship
  of state;
Knowing the patient wisdom how to wait
Until the sands to hour of action ran.
How would our conduct fall beneath thy ban—
We who but lately fought, with hearts elate,
To free the world from evils of old date
And carry through our great Republic's plan!

Ah! couldst thou see us as we are today—
Our careless lust for pleasure and for gold,
Our narrow selfishness, the swift decay
Of leadership that thou wouldst have us hold—
Thou wouldst rebuke us for our shallow aims,
With kindly sorrow, as a father blames!

[August 14, 1909]

IN many ways our America is like Plato's Athens, only with the city a nation. The passion for novelty, the feverish movement, the demagogic misleading of the people—all are here, on larger scale, as they were there. So Plato's bitter reaction against it all, back to the placid changelessness of Egypt, should warn us. One should not look upon the evils of one's time so closely and continuously as to lose trust in the deeper meaning and potentialities of its life.

LEADERSHIP

[Orchard Hill, August 8, 1922]

THIS age of machinery has obscured the significance of leadership, to the point that one hears on every side the assertion that progress is no longer to depend upon leaders, but will result from organization and the action of groups and masses of men.

Such views are utterly wrong. It is just in this age of machinery and materialism that high leadership is most needed, and at the same time most difficult to develop. The price the leader pays is too sadly high: the "white light that beats upon a throne" is nothing in comparison to the garish search-light that plays ceaselessly upon every leader of democracy. The temporary decline of leadership is, indeed, one of the ugly symptoms of the age, indicative, not of progress, but of mediocrity and stagnation. With the return to the soul —which must be, if man is to live and go forward—lofty leadership will arise again, and be increasingly important with each step in the development of democracy.

It is men and women who are eternally the final capital of any nation—strong, fine, cultivated, independently thinking, consecrated men and women; and the more such persons develop in the mass, the surer will be the arising of outstanding individuals, who may guide, inspire and lead those who are worthy to follow. As such leaders always have been the dynamic energy of moral progress, so will they be increasingly as civilization develops. Thought, love and will are life; all else is tools and equipment.

[Tulsa, Oklahoma, January 17, 1919]

BERNARD SHAW is, indeed, the court fool of democracy. As the king's jester told, to the monarch and his courtiers, bitter truths masked as wit and humor, so, by the same method, our ironic jester tells truths equally bitter, to the many-headed tyrant—the public. He is out of sorts with current civilization; and so forever castigating. If only there were something more constructive beneath the taunting jest!

Shaw is at his best in *Man and Superman;* but as a result, this work merely accentuates one's impression of his fundamental attitude. Though in no sense profound, the drama is lively and interesting. Were the hero taken merely as a charming and eccentric youth, in intellectual revolt against philistinism, the play would be a pleasant bit of social satire.

With the long prose setting—especially the *Revolutionist's Handbook*—it becomes an exposition of bizarre social theories, with just enough truth in them to carry the mass of unfair and destructive criticism.

He who proclaims he is teaching nothing may, after the manner of Socrates, attack everything; but if he be without the constructive earnestness in aim and spirit of Socrates, the result may be subtly harmful.

The criticism of democracy contains enough truth to make its unfairness the more misleading; and it explains why the court fool of democracy failed to rise to the War.

Is it that, like Dagonet dancing among the fallen leaves, Shaw jests brilliantly that he may not weep? What the Irish temperament will do, when irritated by the stupidity and steadfastness of the Anglo-Saxon!

Spring

O SPRING, thou glorious heavenly resur-
    rection!
Thou birth of silence into voice and being!
Death is only sleeping, 'neath the seeming
Lie depths of being, breathing, living, feeling,
The issues vast which span the dreams of time.

[Washington, D. C., June 15, 1919]

ONE gets here a startling sense of the vigor, aspiration and tawdriness of American life. The wide and majestic sweep of Pennsylvania Avenue is marred by masses of ugly structures, erected with no thought or purpose beyond immediate commercial returns. The impressive pile of the Capitol itself has its parts poorly related, the two wings inharmonious with the simpler central structure, its decorations stuck on and the ugly green figure set on top of the lantern of the dome.

The beautiful Congressional Library, as a more recent building, constructed in one period, is well unified; but its solid gray harmony is broken, if you please, by great brown and white striped awnings on all its windows: American utility!

The Capitol grounds are lovely, with luxuriant vegetation; but without a bench or chair anywhere, from which one might quietly enjoy their beauty and the view of the great buildings. Evidently the American idea is to "do" them and move on: a phrase as inelegant in English as it is offensive in the attitude of mind it reveals. There is no provision for

155

leisure in American life, except in the way of titillation, diversion, excitement. O for the quiet cafés of Europe, where with a single cup or glass, one may sit and dream, think, read or write for hours! In place of the penny chairs in the parks, America offers only "Keep off the grass." We have so much to learn, and, as a people, are so unaware of the fact.

Some of the later buildings are artistically planned, harmonious and beautiful; but one feels this is rather a fortunate accident. Still, certain of the very recent structures, such as the Red Cross, D. A. R. and Pan American ones, are veritable gems of art. Perhaps we are learning.

The Patent Office, in its unadorned Doric majesty, is one of the most satisfying structures, old or new, in Washington.

Everywhere statues to generals, none to individual soldiers, who bore the brunt of battle and paid the price. Brains, leadership must count; but heroism and sacrifice deserve recognition, in low places as in high. When will the "Sons of Martha" come into their own?

LIFE THE ONE REALITY

[Chicago, December, 1918]

HOW one reacts on one's generalizations in the presence of the stream of life. Defined differences of sex, epoch and race, which seem to hold for the average: how these are obliterated when the tide rolls high in some splendid individual of either sex and any time. Life—rich, full, manifold, infinite in potentiality, overflowing definitions and classifications— it is the one reality.

A Sunset On Lake Ontario

THY sleep in the ocean waves cometh
    apace,
Farewell, farewell to thee, Phœbus Apollo;
Thy hours have finished another day's race,
Farewell, farewell to thee, Phœbus Apollo.

Into the vast abyss sinketh the day,
Farewell, farewell to thee, Phœbus Apollo;
Still but relentless it swept on its way,
Farewell, farewell to thee, Phœbus Apollo.

In the heavens thou leavest a glory of light,
Farewell, farewell to thee, Phœbus Apollo;
While afar in the East ascendeth the night,
Farewell, farewell to thee, Phœbus Apollo.

What do we know of the day or the night?
Farewell, farewell to thee, Phœbus Apollo;
How vain, how vain is our farthest strained
    sight,
Farewell, farewell to thee, Phœbus Apollo.

We sit by the waves as they sweep on the shore,
Farewell, farewell to thee, Phœbus Apollo;
What does it mean that they cease nevermore?
Farewell, farewell to thee, Phœbus Apollo.

Is our longing in vain, our hope but a dream?
Farewell, farewell to thee, Phœbus Apollo;
Is the light of our love but a vanishing gleam?
Farewell, farewell to thee, Phœbus Apollo.

The glory is gone, and gray is the sky,
Farewell, farewell to thee, Phœbus Apollo;
The wind in the trees is a whispering sigh,
Farewell, farewell to thee, Phœbus Apollo.

Our struggles are still, we turn to the night,
Farewell, farewell to thee, Phœbus Apollo;
With the gloom on our hearts we wait for the
    light,
Farewell, farewell to thee, Phœbus Apollo.

ONE by one the brown leaves fall. A sudden gust of wind, and they swirl down and eddy across the ground. Bare gray boughs stretch out against a grayer sky. Down the valley drifts a chill mist. The gray twilight coldly deepens into the homeless night.

[New York City, June 22, 1911]

I HAVE seen Bernhardt again, and for the last time; going once more to *Camille*, to discover whether it would be possible to revise the old impressions of Bernhardt's work. They were merely deepened and accentuated by the pathetic devices through which she strove to conceal age. Never once during the play was one conscious of Camille; but always of Bernhardt acting Camille and displaying Bernhardt. The actress seemed more the courtezan than her subject: one felt the Camille of the story to be far higher in type than the woman Bernhardt portrayed.

The supporting company was composed of singularly unattractive persons; whose chief artistic excellence was facile and accurate rendering of the French lines. One wonders at the tremendous vogue of Bernhardt and her company during the season. Is it due to the American worship for one who has achieved?

Field Flowers

THE violet blushes before the rose,
  Reigning, the queen of flowers;
No daisy can vie with the lily that blows
In the fragrance of summer bowers;

But the purple eyes of the violet yearn,
'Mid the grass, with a gentler grace;
From roses and lilies fair, we turn
To the daisy or pansy face.

These are not poems of epic art
Nor stage-moulded drama forms;
But thoughts and moods of the inner heart,
Born of its calms and storms.

They are violets, pansies, sprung from the sod,
Or daisies, perchance wind-sown;
But the hand that scattered the seed was
    God—
The seed that to thoughts has grown.

Rosemary, pansies, heart's-ease, rue:
These are my garden flowers;
Memories, thoughts and responses true:
These are my blossomed hours.

Then take them, not as a master work,
But broken bits of song—
Thoughts that in lonely forests lurk
Or brood o'er the human throng.

[Orchard Hill, September 4, 1920]

THIS chapter of life is too short: if only one had more time; yet how we waste the time we have! The days slip by, and always one dreams that the next turn in the road will bring the quiet landscape where one may rest the spirit.

Thus with most human beings life is in expectation rather than achievement. Always the realization seems just beyond. Today is poor; but tomorrow——! So we postpone; and the opportunity of the day is lost. To live each moment: that is the rarely understood, still more rarely applied, secret.

The chasm is wide between active leisure of the spirit and enforced idleness; yet it takes only self-direction and inner resource to turn the latter into the former. To "garner the sheaf of wisdom": surely, through all the disappointments, loneliness and endless driving work, that may be achieved.

[Montclair, N. J., July 27, 1909]

IT is an impressive experience to read in the same time the *Letters* of St. Jerome and those of Goethe. Not a little of Goethe's warmly human temperament is in St. Jerome; but how widely contrasting is the life-view. Poor Jerome—with such human capacities; yet convinced that only by destroying the natural life could he be in high degree pleasing to God! His account of his delight in reading Cicero and other Latins, and of the severe rebuke of his sin that came to him in a vision, almost makes one weep. The strange reverence for the negative purity of physical virginity: holding even widows to be far below the virgins, in the estimation and love of God: how strangely remote and even perverse it all is; and yet, for how much unnecessary human suffering the superstition is accountable.

Then the swing of the pendulum the other way; and the strange use of the sensuously voluptuous imagery of the *Song of Songs* to express the relation of the dedicated virgin to Christ. In reprimanding a mother for objecting to her daughter's vow of perpetual virginity, he says, "You are the mother-in-law of God"!—Ah, Ah!

How subtle the consequences of the old superstition are: ramifying in all our finer life, making many a sensitive woman ashamed of the womanhood that should be her pride, and blemishing with the stigma of evil the sweetest garment the spirit may wear. The further consequence—the confusion of all standards of sex-morality—if not to be charged wholly to the one superstition, nevertheless follows naturally, as the pendulum swings from unwise repression of the natural life to its careless and uncontrolled affirmation. In the end, develops the foolish situation, where a hard and fast line of churchly sanction is drawn: all on one side being acclaimed as virtue; all on the other condemned as vice.

Parting

THE sun may shine
   Or the winds may moan,
The clouds rest still
Or in storms be blown;
But forever and all
You are my own;
Forever and all I love you, Dear,
Forever and all I love you.

Although life's path
Give naught but pain,
Though all my hopes
May be in vain,
E'en though we never
Should meet again,
Forever and all I love you, Dear,
Forever and all I love you.

[Glen Hill Farm. August 10. 1911]

LIVE from the will. *Choose* life at each step and in each detail. This does not mean fanaticism nor the sordid calculation of moments: it is wholly consistent with a splendid abandonment to the great things of life. It does mean *choosing* when to abandon, and when to count the cost. It does mean keeping ceaselessly the mastery with the will, and refusing to be led or driven by the accident of circumstances.

[Glen Hill Farm, July 27, 1906]

GOETHE'S life is his most remarkable work of art—greater even than *Faust*. The more one studies the varied expressions of his personality, the more one is amazed at the unity of purpose, consistency of effort and wide range of relation and achievement everywhere displayed. It is true he made many mistakes, frequent wrong choices; and that periods of relative idleness or misdirected effort recur across his years; yet what ever-renewed and long-continued self-control and struggle to realize all the wondrous potentiality within him! With reference to the whole problem of self-culture, his is the most instructive life we are privileged to know intimately.

[Montclair, N. J., July 27, 1909]

IT is amazing that Goethe could portray, at such almost tiresome length, the sentimentality of Werther; and yet free himself so largely from it. The contrast between *Werther* and the letters of Goethe, written to Lotte and Kestner while the book was being composed, is striking. Goethe saw the weakness

169

of whatever sentimentality he had experienced; and wisely and courageously freed himself from it. There is no better evidence of his sanity of spirit.

How full of life he was in the Werther period: he must have given many a longing sigh to Lotte's shrewd German heart! "Klug" war sie: she doubtless saw the danger of life with a man of genius, while acknowledging his compelling charm, and decided on the safer lot with the more prosaic advocate. Then, too, probably Goethe never asked her to break her engagement!

Werther belongs permanently. With all its morbidness, its long drawn out melodramatic sentiment, it voices a permanent phase of human experience. The youth of genius will always show something of its mood at some point of development; and genius merely experiences, in acute form, what is characteristic of youth generally. In some epochs the fever is more hectic, in others it is scarcely to be marked; but the tendency is in all life.

[Glen Hill Farm, July 21, 1906]

THE *Italian Journey* pulsates with Goethe's wonderful personality, as youthful in response to new influences as in the early years revealed in the *Autobiography*. His sedulous use of time is instructive: like all others, he had continually to spur himself on. The separate days often seemed wasted, so far short did he fall of his aim and plan; but in the years, his achievement is incomparable.

His remarkable worldly shrewdness, verging at times on a peculiar form of selfishness, also appears; yet was he not right to place his own life and achievement first, avoiding relationships which would distract and dissipate?

In this work, as everywhere, his life-wisdom astonishes. The pages are strewn with wise sayings, summing up a principle of personal conduct or sheering down into the heart of experience. As a philosopher, he is in another world from the system-makers, who elaborate their sterile theories in the study, remote from the vibrant life of man. Since Plato, with the possible exception of Emerson, no such wealth of insight has been uttered.

The episode with the Milan lady reminds

one of the Friederike and Charlotte stories, only Goethe has grown more prudent with the years, and stops earlier in the history; yet would not he have been wiser, had he given free rein to his natural impulse and married the Milan lady, instead of going home to take up with Christiane Vulpius? Does not a certain extreme of worldly wisdom over-reach itself; while a more generous self-abandonment may, sometimes, find the way of life?

If only Goethe could have recognized that in personal relationship, as in art, one must ever worship at the shrine of the Goddess of Limits; that bonds of feeling, gladly accepted and lived, bless and further, instead of dwarfing, the true development of genius.

Christmas Eve

ONE year ago the children slept,
  While you and I, with laughter free,
Placed gifts upon the Christmas-tree:
  Tonight again the children sleep—
I did not dream that I should weep
Tonight beside the Christmas-tree.

I lean my head upon my hands,
There is no heartease with the rue—
What is there left for me to do?
  My eyes are filled with blinding tears,
I can but dream of dear dead years,
But weep alone and dream of you.

[July 24, 1911]

FOR what is it all: the pain, struggle, aspiration and failure? That question is ever beneath all our thinking, and beats its way up increasingly into consciousness. The conviction that love and wisdom are alone in themselves worth while, and that life is to be measured in terms of these, is no less strong; but life appears sadly ineffective. So much of the gain *seems* to be lost, with the mental and physical decay of age; and then—the annulling shadow! One must believe that the gain is *not* lost—one clings increasingly to the conviction of immortality, of the eternity of personality; but how much is dark!

[Glen Hill Farm, August 22, 1906]

WORK is life's sake—not life for work's sake. The man who cripples his life, foregoing what he should accept, that he may get on more comfortably with the world in vocational adjustment, is making the means, the end, and sinning against his own soul.

FRONTIER COUNTRY

[Tahlequah, Okla., June 16, 1921]

THIS is, indeed, frontier country: crude conditions of life, hastily built farm houses, carelessly dressed people, fertile soil inadequately cultivated. Nevertheless, it is a thriving, prosperous world, hardly aware of the business depression so wide-spread over the land.

The brilliant sky and intense sun are like Italy; but there all likeness ends. How wonderful it would be if, in place of these ugly rambling buildings, there were here the cool arcades and artistic structures of Italy! It could just as well be, if only there were the instinctive love and desire for beauty. How much we have to learn as a people, and how our complacent arrogance prevents our realizing the fact!

[May 30, 1914]

T HAT pessimism should be the inspiration of naturalism can be due only to the sickness of the modern spirit. Good is no less "natural" than evil, joy than sorrow, life than death. When will appear another great genial spirit, broad in appreciation of life, balanced in creation, who will show again that *all man's life* is natural, portraying the good and the evil, the joy and the tragedy, in the whole mystery of existence? When such a master appears, the fog of pessimism will evaporate; the nightmare figures, born of the half-truths of the mist, will vanish; the sunlight will be as natural as the rayless dark; and man will stand again whole and mysterious, with hope as well as despair in him, joy sharing with sorrow the empire of his breast.

Shakespeare and Goethe, return!

The Lady Of Lake Lucerne

[A ballad of the 16th Century]

ONEVERMORE will the sunlight beam
With the calm of long ago;
O never in peace will the last rays gleam
O'er the mountains wreathed in snow;

Never again can the silvery moon
Shine o'er a still lake's breast;
For in troubled whispers the waters croon,
Filled with a vague unrest.

Across the bosom of Lake Lucerne
The last low sun-rays fall;
While softens the crest of the mountains stern,
The moonlight's silvery pall;

The boat glides swiftly o'er the lake
That lies in such calm peace:
But when to love, the heart-deeps wake,
The passion can never cease.

Rowed with his regular, easy stroke,
The boat sped over the lake;

The calm of the waters only broke
To the ripple left in the wake.

With a far-off look in her dreaming eyes,
The woman gazed at the shore:
The dread of some sudden dark surprise
Brooding her spirit o'er.

"O Lover mine, why didst thou leave
Thy refuge safe in the North;
Will thy cruel foes my life bereave
Of all that gives it worth?

"Thou art hunted on every mountain slope,
Ah, why didst thou return!
And yet, we can die, if there be no hope,
And with death, their vengeance spurn.

"For thee alone my soul was born,
And liveth alone in thee;
What then, if thou from my clinging torn,
Shouldst die for this hour with me!"

O passion, that o'er the fond heart sweeps,
As gale ne'er swept o'er the sea:
How thy breath, in the spirit's deeps,
Tears with its agony!

THE LADY OF LAKE LUCERNE

"O Heart for whom my heart doth yearn,
Thy dread is a woman's fear:
We are crossing the waters of Lake Lucerne,
The southern shore is near.

"Tomorrow's moon will shine in peace,
O'er the calm lake's silent shore;
While we, afar, shall find release
From fear forevermore."

A wan smile played o'er her death-pale face,
A long sigh broke from her heart:
"Ah Dear, could I hold thee in close embrace,
In a nook from the world apart!

"O never again will the silvery moon
Shine down on thee and me:
Like the mournful words of an ancient rune,
Is my heart's dread prophecy."

The boat to the white sands lightly drew,
Like a ghost from the nether gloom——
But ah! the woman's instinct true
That felt the coming doom——

A flash; her wild despairing cry;
And at her feet he lay:

"Ah Love, Love, must I then die
At the dawn of promised day!"

With tender woman's hand she pushed
The boat back from the shore;
In vain the ambushed murderers rushed—
The space grew more and more.

The sword still lay by the dead man's side—
Love, ah love is woe—
The living flood, in a crimson tide,
Flowed o'er her breast of snow.

O'er Lake Lucerne a tempest swept;
Amidst the billows' roar,
The blinding flare of the lightning leapt—
The boat was seen no more.

Ah love, love, that thou canst rend
The heart with thy passion so;
Ah love, love, that thou canst end
In such despair and woe!

Ne'er can the moon so peaceful gleam
As in the long ago;
Ne'er can the sun in quiet seem
To sink from the peaks of snow;

THE LADY OF LAKE LUCERNE

For over the waters of Lake Lucerne,
In the evening's hush and still,
A moan and a sigh are breathed, that turn
The heart with a death-like chill.

O some have sung of war and state,
And some of courts and kings;
Some like the dove to its cooing mate,
And some as the wild thrush sings;

But the theme that makes the hot tears start,
With the pity of God above,
Is the passion that fills a woman's heart
And the depths of a woman's love!

[Vredeoord, June 6, 1914]

IT is difficult to keep life simple and follow the straight path of one's own convictions, since the one person is bound, by all sorts of subtle and complicated ties, to so many others. One seems tangled in a web of relations; and the single strand cannot determine the color and texture of the whole cloth. It is hard to see how the individual can make his life express exactly his own convictions, except by Thoreau's rigid and selfish exclusion of all relations.

IN all work that concerns other persons one must accept elements of failure, since there can be no such thing as perfect success. Therein is the limitation and pain of the teacher, parent, reformer, preacher, as compared with sculptor, painter, poet, musician, or even artisan. Thus the wisdom of the first group is to look across life; accepting faults that cannot be conquered, and welcoming any measure of success possible. Hard lesson to learn!

183

What Is In Your Hearts, My Children?

WHAT is in your hearts, my children?
    Do you aspire, as I did at your years?
Are your minds filled with dreams and high
    aims,
Of which I cannot know,
As mine was, while those about me
Could not understand?
    Or are you still asleep,
Content with today's joy
And lured by the moment?
    Would I might know!
    Have I failed to touch in you
The springs of ambition—
To waken the vision
That makes one ever strive?
    Ah, how alone at last one's life is,
How helpless all the yearning
To touch and mould another soul!

[June 17, 1921]

SLOWLY we are coming to recognize that in all problems of industry and society, in every phase of social readjustment the basic factor is the psychological one—the human attitude.

We found out in the War that the foundation on which everything else rests, is the morale of the army and the people behind the army. It was, indeed, the break-down of the German morale, first in the people at home, then in the armies in the field, that ended the War; and until that break, the end could not come.

Morale is just as fundamental in peace as in war, in business and industry as in the fighting quality of an army. The full recognition of this will be a long step toward humanism.

CENTRALIZED GOVERNMENT

[July 4, 1921]

SO many persons who are thinking on the current problems want to settle them all, on short notice, by centralized governmental action, from the top, down. The method is speciously attractive; but it is utterly wrong and antithetical to democracy. Its results would be a partly tyrannical, partly paternalistic beaurocracy of politicians, constantly interfering with economic laws, destroying initiative, discouraging free cooperation, and stultifying the development of free men and women. This fatal tendency must be fought in every aspect of American life: above all, in industry and education.

[Massillon, O., April 17, 1921]

GAUTIER'S *Mademoiselle de Maupin* is a bad book. The cult of beauty is all very well, and needed by our philistine society; but here it is not the healthy Greek love of beauty, but the modern perverse cultivation of the flesh, by an idle and decadent class.

Idle persons, living on inherited wealth, with no vocation but capricious pleasure-seeking, swiftly are corrupted; and, indeed, have no right to live on the earth. The cult of beauty can never be rightly attained, except by those who work hard, with a high purpose in life.

That *Mademoiselle de Maupin* made an epoch in George Moore's life, is a sufficient criticism and estimate of George Moore.

There is much beautiful and clever writing in the book, but for what? To break down the instinct of personal loyalty, stimulate perverse desires, and eliminate the soul from the beauty that is its garment, love from the passion that is its vocabulary: Decadence!

PATERNALISM

[Glen Hill Farm, August 15. 1909]

IT is surprising how many influences in America at present tend to the drifting away from democracy, toward the belief in governing the people from above by kindly force and pleasant deception. The loose application of the general theory of evolution gave the first great impetus in that direction, doing away subtly with the older theory of equality and the rights of man. Then came the immense and rapid increase of wealth, with the consequent segregation of different social groups. The evident breakdown of democracy in practice, in so many aspects, increased the distrust of its forms and methods. Finally, a half-developed science of Sociology, drawing its inspiration largely from German writers, bred on German beaurocracy and imperialism, organized into theory the reaction against the older American institutions and beliefs. The situation is perilous; and the peril is accentuated by the fact that the drifting is so unconscious, and the intellectual reaction so arrogant.

[January 10, 1919]

I AM impressed with Lafcadio Hearn's statement to his Japanese students that the one indispensable condition of their appreciation of English literature was to recognize the fact that Western civilization centers on the "worship" of woman. That is true; and it is the great line of cleavage between the East and the West. It is significant that the result is a far saner and healthier civilization in the Occident than in the Orient.

What will be the effect of the widely successful feminist movement on that civilization? Will it tend to eliminate, or at least weaken, the worship of woman? If so, what then will be the future of the fine flower of Western life?

[June 27, 1921]

THE cult of love and woman in the middle age was a strange and wonderful development. Italy was torn with ceaseless warfare, carried on with barbaric cruelty. Life was wild and chaotic; yet in the midst of it rises this delicate, spiritual worship of woman as the pure guiding star of life. The finer feminine virtues were created by this noble chivalry. Did it mean the soul saving itself, in the midst of barbaric coarse action: an instinctive recovery of the balance of the spirit?

That Dante's *Vita Nuova* could be produced in the middle age is a supreme illustration at once of the wide vitality of its life and of the spiritual height it was capable of achieving.

The school of Italian love poets is almost an exotic flower, such as we expect in the most highly refined phases of purely modern culture. O life is one in all ages!

Her Kiss

DID you ever lift to your lips a rose,
All wet with the morning dew;
Kissing the heart that its petals close
And breathing its fragrance new?

O then the secret perhaps you'll guess—
Though an image faint is this—
Of my Darling's gift of happiness
In the wonder of her kiss.

Dear mouth like a flower upturned to mine,
Lips wet with warm desire,
And parted trembling, in tender sign
Of the glowing of love's fire!

An instant I bend o'er the flower sweet—
The passion-flower of bliss;
And then—ah the love and joy complete
In the wonder of her kiss!

[On train, June 26, 1921]

I T is a joy to take up deeply the study of
Dante again.   His lofty thinking takes one
into the atmosphere of the eternal problems,
far removed from the harassing complexities
on the surface of this time.   This, with the
majesty of his imagery and the beauty of his
melody, exercises the same lifting power over
the spirit that the high mountains have.   One
breathes more deeply and looks out over a
wider vision of life.

Dante's grim, and sometimes light, humor
appeals to me as never before; as does the
feminine sweetness of his melody, in contrast
to the smiting vigor of his art.

Dante "builds the lofty rhyme," where
Shakespeare pours out his wealth of beauty
with free spontaneity.   Dante chisels, where
Shakespeare sings.

[Greeley, Colorado, June 28, 1921]

O NE of the amazing powers of Dante is
his masculine influence on other minds,
fertilizing them and causing them to bring forth
fruitfully.   This is an evidence of the very
highest type of intellectual and artistic power.

Francesca da Rimini, for instance, has given birth to a dozen dramas. Dante's account of the heroic last voyage of Ulysses is the inspiration of Tennyson's *Ulysses* and Lowell's *Columbus;* his Sordello gave Browning's poem.

Dante is full of such vivid and inspiring characterizations: Pia, Statius, Ugolino, Farinata, the elder Cavalcanti, Filippo Argenti, Cacciaguida, Matilda: they are everywhere: portraits etched with a pen dipped in fire; painted with the warm colors of Nature; created on a background of light multiplied into light: how they all live!

IT is the test of supreme imagination in art that described experiences are accepted as real. Dante has this power in superlative degree. Dealing with supernatural material, as he does, one never questions the steps of his pilgrimage as actually taken. His meeting with Statius, for instance, is so life-like and with such a delightful touch of humor, that one is sure their conversation really took place on a terrace of the purifying mountain.

193

With Some Carnations

THE warm spice-odor of these fragrant
    flowers
But hints the wondrous perfume of your
    hair;
Their glorious color, fading with the hours,
Is pale beside the beauty that you wear.

I send them to you, full of love-thoughts,
    Sweet—
Forever blooming in your beauty's dower—
I bend in constant worship at your feet,
You, radiant with love-light, dear human
    flower!

[Odin, Illinois, June 17, 1919]

A QUEER, little, commonplace village in the middle of this fat state—a mere railroad junction for two important lines.

A coal miner, stoop-shouldered, lamp in cap, goes by. A collarless young engineer hastens from the little hotel. A sad-faced French girl, with tubercular cough, moves restlessly on the hotel porch, and then sits with drawn face and closed eyes. A farmer's boy, hauling a plow and a bundle of hay; a tender, but commonplace middle-aged man, helping his sick wife into the dining-room: Life—it is all here!

[Vredeoord, July 4, 1914]

HOW blindly lavish youth is; maturity how vainly regretful! Youth is conscious of stores of life that seem inexhaustible. These are poured out carelessly for such slight ends. Then, when the man finds the rocks multiply in his path and feels the need for all his resources to struggle forward, he discovers the trembling hand and the body worn so that it can no longer leap enthusiastically to the task. Youth spends recklessly; age mourns without avail!

[Vredeoord, June 3, 1914]

STRANGE, how archaic much of Emerson seems, read today. At times, too, he descends to a chattiness that is almost trivial. His greatest work is in the first half of his career. No subsequent volume equalled the *First Series of Essays* or *Nature*. The increase of mannerisms is noticeable in the late work. Nevertheless, one bows to the permanent worth of his great thoughts and the fidelity with which he kept to his own thinking.

It is interesting to find Emerson, with all his optimism, almost despairing of American politics and passing scathing criticisms on all aspects of American life. Practically every complaint we have to lodge today, he makes. His attitude toward American politics is identical with Plato's toward Athenian democracy. Is it not the permanent attitude of the thinker toward the seething ephemeralities on the surface of life?

One has only to read consecutively in Emerson, for a considerable time, to realize his limitations in thought as well as form. Whole ranges of human experience are a sealed book to him; just as the qualities that go to organizing a masterpiece are wanting in his art. He tended the altar fire with steadfast consecration. He observed faithfully, and gathered the fruit with persistent reflection. He had rare power in phrasing the pregnant apothegm. He was better than his philosophy, for his New England inheritance and puritan instincts saved him from the practical consequences of his Over-Soul theory. Annulling distinctions, advocating quiescence, holding the equivalency of all actions, influences and experiences, in relation to the Over-Life: all this is dangerous doctrine for any but an already formed Puritan. Emerson's mysticism is a healthy reaction on Calvinism; but character exists by definition and distinction; achievement results, not from letting go, but from self-direction and self-control. Emerson *taught* chiefly the background of reception, while he *lived* the foreground of effort. One wonders how far his teaching may be responsible for various complacent weaknesses in phases of "New Thought."

Edinburgh Castle

THE stream of human life flows heedless
    on
Through avenues where lofty mansions stand,
And through dim alleys where the old town
    lies
And quaint tall houses lift their time-stained
    fronts.
Above it all the ancient castle glooms,
Crowning with dark-gray stone the grass-
    grown rocks.
Think how within it human passions throbbed!
Queen Mary's womanhood with its great thirst
For power and love and joy; the sainted
    Queen's
Religious fervor, still ensymboled by
The little chapel with its lowly roof.

The sombre beauty of the castle still
Looks down o'er winding streets and houses
    tall;
But where are now the human hearts that beat,
That loved and hated, thirsted and enjoyed?

EDINBURGH CASTLE

The stream of human life flows heedless on,
Loving and hating in the mansion hall
And in the dim old houses of the town,
Craving today as in forgotten years.

[Chicago, December 13, 1918]

ONE feels, in the public everywhere, the desire to be lifted away from the long strain of thinking on the War and the immense problems it has produced. That thinking must go on through the years of difficult reconstruction; but the deeper need, now coming to consciousness, is to return to the eternal problems of human life and to the healing and exalting influence of beauty. The great masters—Dante, Shakespeare, Goethe, Browning—are coming to their own again, and the popular mind responds to them with new keen appreciation.

The Lost Cause

ACROSS the heavens swept the wonderful
    milky way,
Marvelously alight with its dust of a million
    worlds;
Over the dusky mountains the Pleiades' femi-
    nine beauty
Gladdened the eastern sky with a soft and
    delicate light.
Under them like a moon shone the brilliant
    lamp of Saturn,
While over the mountains' crest Orion still
    slept in the dark.
The moon had long since sunk in the waves of
    the western ocean;
Yet wonderful seemed the night alight with its
    myriad stars.
On and on we swept in our wildly furious rid-
    ing;
The mountains seemed to retreat like a mystic
    and ghostly host;
Only a watch dog's howl broke the silence
    about us,

Silence that weighed us down with a sense of
    coming doom.
The restless breath of the ocean sent the mist-
    fog into the valley;
One by one the stars were lost in the shrouding
    gloom.
Swiftly and silently moving, soon its breath
    was upon us,
Touching our burning cheeks with its moist and
    chilly kiss.
Who shall tell the end of the horrible ride in
    the mist-fog?
Our cause was lost and the hosts of the enemy
    closed around.
He fell, my hero-friend, and I was made their
    captive,
To lie here alone in the dark, chained in this
    prison cell.
O for a breath of air and a sight of the vast
    of heaven,
A glimpse of the glorious night alight with its
    shining stars!
O to have died with him a hero's death in the
    battle,
Rather than grieve alone in this silent
    prison tomb!

[June 24, 1919]

TWO tendencies, directly resulting from the activities and experiences of the War, menace our democracy, particularly in the field of education. The first is the over-centralization in all aspects of government. The Federal Bureau of Education has increased its power and has its hand on the schools of the nation as never before; while other government agencies multiply the centralized control.

There will soon be an inevitable attempt to standardize the entire country; which would mean a dead average level, absentee beaurocratic control, and the paralyzing of local initiative. This is the reverse of democracy, which must pay the price of irregularity and frequent inefficiency, to preserve free initiative, voluntary cooperation and effort from below.

The closely allied danger is that, having found how easy it is to mould public opinion by organized effort, we may seek to use the powerful government agencies for direct propaganda of opinions. Then, with a better motive, we should make Germany's mistake.

Democracy must seek to awaken, emancipate and inform the popular mind, *never* to stamp it with a prearranged system of ideas.

[Boise, Idaho, June 20, 1912]

HUMOR is the one grace that saves from fanaticism. Without it, one is apt to take all things, little and great, on the same plane of importance, and so to treat with equal seriousness the whim of opinion and the conviction at the heart. Humor is the other side of ethical good taste, and without it no one can lead a truly moral life.

The City

THE surging stream of human life flows
  through the streets of the city:
A sweeping sea of faces, all with the same hu-
  man nature,
And yet each different from the rest:
Some stolidly unawakened, untouched by the
  joy and the thrill of life;
Some sensually depraved through long, long
  obedience to beastly instincts;
Some hungering for the joy of life,
That has been glimpsed only to be forever de-
  nied.
Painted women heavily and sensually self-sat-
  isfied;
Men with the wild gambling instinct
Written in every line of their haggard and de-
  based faces;
Curious loiterers who turn to hear the street-
  car driver
Whistle at a stubborn teamster who blocks the
  way;
Dissipated men who lounge about the corners,

Staring rudely and vulgarly at the women who
    pass;
Children with the light of Heaven in their
    sweet faces,
As yet unspoiled by the hard brutality of the
    world;
Girls with sweet innocent eyes, glowing with
    the first light of awakening love;
And others whose looks betoken only too
    plainly
Familiarity with the hard and debasing half-
    knowledge of the vulgar world.
Each in the seemingly aimless throng pressing
    on toward his own goal,
Seeking life and joy as these appear to him,
Heedless of all others, excepting here and
    there a single unit
In the great surging sea.

So the sweeping stream of life
Flows through the streets of the City:
Swirling on in the moment of light,
Which, for each soul in the throng,
Lies between two dark and not understood eter-
    nities.

[July 7, 1919]

THROUGH the "glories" of the wars of ambition of Louis XIV and the ensuing persistent league of nations against him, France was so exhausted that she sank from the leadership of Europe to the position of a second rate power; yet by the close of the century she had so recovered as to be all but invincible in the Revolution and under Napoleon.

The chances for Germany's swift recovery are even greater. What will the world see fifty years from now: a brotherhood of free peoples, or another and fiercer attempt at world empire?

How quickly nations can pass from grandeur and leadership to ruin and insignificance, and from obscurity to domination. That is one reason it is so dangerous to attempt to guarantee the existing order.

The seventeenth Century is an almost unbroken record of wars—wars of greed, ambition, intrigue. Louis XIV attempted, with less brutality and efficiency, much that the Hohenzollerns have just tried. It is not that Wilhelm II had not plenty of historic precedents: it was that he was an anachronism, attempting the crimes of the past in an age that will not endure them. All governments take notice!

How faintly President Wilson announces the new order of things, now that the Peace Conference is behind, compared to the glowing promises he made before going to Paris. Of course it was too much to hope that the world could be made over suddenly. It was to be expected that old jealousies and methods would reassert themselves; but surely, after the bitter lesson, we shall not go back to the old order of intrigue, thieving diplomacy and wars of envy and aggression. For the moment the President is as much discredited, as previously his power to make the world over was foolishly overrated—perhaps, in some measure, by himself. History will recognize that he did rather more than could have been expected, and that a long step forward has been taken.

A Thunder Shower

DEEP cloud rumbles, like firing of distant
   guns,
A darkening shadow over the lush grass;
A waiting mood—only a bird calling anxiously.
   The cloud battle drawing nearer:
A blinding flash and instant deafening roar;
Then a sweep of fierce-driven rain,
Guttering the roads, and drenching through the
      windows.
   The great guns slowly withdrawing;
The heavy firing again a distant growl of
      the sky,
Sinking to silence.
Peace in the cool, windless air;
The grass and the foliage brilliant in fresh-
      washed green:
   Only a passing summer storm.

PIERRE LOTI

[Vredeoord, August 23, 1915]

YES, Loti's *Rarahu* still exercises its spell —not quite so strong as a dozen years ago, perhaps, and with a sense of something fictitious in the story—but still beautiful and strong. My judgment of it is the same—as of Loti and the significance of his life.

A new France is coming—regenerated by heroic struggle, with a new spiritual life. Will it mean a fresh flowering of the wonderful French genius in beautiful art?

How human life renews itself in most unexpected fashion: the old epoch is gone; the nineteenth century is as remote as the eighteenth; what will the new age bring forth?

[Chicago, December 7, 1920]

LOTI'S *Pilgrim of Angkor* has all his descriptive powers and beauty of language; but that is all. There is no interpretation of life in it, and the reflections upon the transciency of man grow a little monotonous. It is creative power, as contrasted with receptive and descriptive power, he fundamentally lacks.

The closing passage, on the Pity Supreme, indicates, after all, a faith under his persistent skepticism, a faith that only the withdrawal of age could enable him to formulate and accept. The Æolian harp, that has vibrated to so many winds of beauty and desire, draws to silence with the grave over-tone of the soul!

In Memory of Mrs. J. E. M.

[June 10, 1922]

A SPIRIT buoyant and a vision wide,
A friend devoted and a mother true;
An eagerness that would not be denied,
Quick humor and an interest ever new:

She saw her children filling places high
And serving well the nation's deeper need:
Her life fulfilled, she did not fear to die,
But followed where the silent voices lead.

HOW strange are the adjustments and compensations of the spirit: the deepest pain tends to wear itself out; the most acute anguish ends in numbness; lost realities are replaced by spiritual theories; and for the life and joy that are wanting is substituted the figment of a dream. Let it not be so with me!

[Kansas City, Mo., June 15, 1921]

STRANGE—the fascination of the esoteric, and the pity is it takes just the minds least balanced and equipped with solid scientific training to deal with it safely and wisely. It is true, "There are more things in heaven and earth than are dreamt of" in our philosophy; but we would better master what is clearly this side the borderland, before attempting to cross it. There is so much we may know, clearly and definitely, and that as yet we do not know: better learn that first!

[Atlanta, Ga., April 26, 1914]

WOMEN exercise tremendous driving force upon men; but comparatively few women, unless deeply influenced by religion, care much how the success is won, so that the man succeeds. What the man "aspired to be, and was not," seldom "comforts" the woman. She wants results, and usually tangible ones. When a woman does rise to forgive a man for failure, that is due to her maternal nature —in that she is mother rather than comrade.

Does this situation result from the fact that women have so much the harder lot? A woman may have high ambitions and aspirations; but she finds herself tied to the fortunes of a man. She can mould him, of course; but often he is such poor clay. His success is ease and opportunity for her; his failure is hardship and limitation; yet once having accepted him, there is, except through disloyalty, rarely any escape. Men will; women influence. Men fight; women wait the issue. Men, may, sometimes, make themselves; women are often made by the circumstances of their husbands. No wonder so many women believe in Fate!

217

The Life Stake

ON the roulette-board of Destiny I gambled my years,
"Rouge-et-noir," and the little ball rolled.
I won small pieces—hours all of gold,
But never the great prize.

On the roulette-board of Destiny I gambled
my years—
All my years, and now I am old.
My poor gains are all like a story retold,
That gives no surprise.

On the roulette-board of Destiny I gambled
my years,
It is done—the sad player is cold—
Were it better I had been either more or less
bold?
What then—when hope dies?

[Glen Hill Farm, August 28, 1908]

THE world is usually vain and wrong in judging lives great and small, and fails utterly to grasp the true significance of the deeps of personal life. Where the great man, however, compels by his genius final acceptance of his life, the lesser man fails of this, and goes down to what is apparently defeat. Thus his lot, if the less widely scandalized, is the more painful; and it is most important that he who dares break with the world's established order, in his personal life, should strive to achieve, in his vocation, work so high as to compel recognition of his sincerity, and, in the end, acceptance of himself. Thus the artist who leaves what is permanent is fortunate beside his equally radical compeer who works in more evanescent fields. All this anent Wagner and Goethe as men and artists!

[On train, Wyoming, June 30, 1915]

WHAT a mass of poor stuff gets printed in the magazines, answering the mere desire for distraction, for the transient titillation of the imagination. That desire results from the same lack of inner culture and resource that sends people travelling, in the search for ever new and changing sensations to stimulate a jaded and vacant mind.

Great literature will come again only when we have acquired true leisure of spirit, in no way dependent on external environment and often least evident where the surrounding conditions seem most restful. Thus he who is wise will seek to attain that leisure of the spirit, without waiting for changed conditions, in the midst of the bewildering kaleidoscope of current life. Repose in the solitary and silent temple of one's own spirit: that is the solution.

IT is a sign of health—if crude health—in the American people, that they demand a happy ending to drama and novel. It is childish, of course, to refuse to face bitter truths; but to see only evil and pain in life is a symptom of moral degeneration. Youth and health make faith easy; but *faith* is the first condition of lasting health and youthfulness of spirit.

IT is the French who can write. Their inexorable tradition of style gives even mediocre French authors a distinction, wanting in some of our best. American writers most of all need style—finished mastery of accurate and beautiful English—equivalent to the average skill of European authors; and then we shall be ready to begin great work.

[Oklahoma City, June 25, 1921]

THE appeal of Shakespeare is perennial and to people of all types. Nowhere else is there such universality nor such marvelous phrasing power.

Apparently Shakespeare did not fully know his gifts. Did he prefer to be an aristocratic gentleman at Stratford, rather than go on creating works of art? Would he have resumed (or continued) writing, after getting settled in the environment at Stratford, had he lived?

It seems impossible to imagine him deliberately and permanently abandoning his creative work at fifty. He is certainly one of the puzzles of history.

[Memphis, Tenn., April 18, 1914]

HOW genial Shakespeare is, compared to such a modern master as Ibsen: one feels health and sanity in all his view of life. It is significant that there is no drama of protest in Shakespeare: everywhere is the constructive portrayal of actual humanity.

Are modern men more fragmentary; or is

life less sincere today?   Have we multiplied
lying conventions; or is the spirit more awake,
so that we are conscious of the limitations and
revolt against them?

THE PROGRAM OF PROGRESS

[Chicago, December 15, 1918]

THERE is enough produced by the machinery of modern civilization for all to have an abundance. The problem is one of just division and distribution. Eliminate unnecessary middle men; force the idle parasites to work or tax them out of existence; treat the hand laborer as a human being, whose whole life-product society takes, and for whose whole life society is, in turn, responsible; never permit labor to be treated as a commodity to be bought and sold; work to replace industrial warfare by cooperation, and class spirit by a fraternity of the whole: these are the basic principles of reconstruction.

Awakening

O SPRING, Spring, thou heavenly birth
    And all unfolding into life
Of forms that grace the gladdened earth,
    With beauty rife.

These months, these days,—these moments,
    yea,
Are my life's spring, since now for me
My night has brightened into day
    And now I see.

THE STUDENT SPIRIT

[Edmond, Okla., June, 1919]

THE nineteen hundred young people studying here represent a whole world of aspiration, energy, hope, selfishness and enthusiasm. Each with a purely personal range of ideals and relations; all thrown together in a common effort for a little while: they are a fair type of humanity.

ONE meets so many young students who seem to have no interest in what they can learn from their courses; but desire only to get through, and secure grades with the least possible effort. Successfully to escape reading a book, they regard as a triumph.

What does this mean? Is it that we have emphasized credits, graduation, degrees so much that the student has lost sight of the real, in the badge; or is it that the student spirit—the desire to know that one may know, to be wise that one may be wise—has almost gone out in the younger generation?

WHAT a country ours is, with wide, still practically limitless opportunity! "A career open to talent, without distinction of birth": Napoleon's motto still holds of our American life. If only the view of life and what it is worth were saner; if only the ambition were for more human ends! The opportunity is endless; the fulfillment often tawdry and vain.

[Boulder, Colorado, August 19, 1920]

OUR people mean well. Their fault is carelessness, preoccupation with selfish ends, not bad intention. The need is for great leadership, to make them see the path and challenge them to follow it. They will respond, now, as in the War.

[Glen Hill Farm, August 28, 1908]

OSCAR WILDE'S preface to *Rose Leaf and Apple Leaf* gives an admirable statement of the "art for art's sake" theory; and shows at once the strength and weakness of the school holding it, as of Wilde's own work. The thesis is far too narrow: it does not fit the facts. That beauty of execution is the chief thing, is true of Wilde's poetry; but that it is the only thing is not true, even there. It is the expression of human life that gives to the preliminary sonnet and closing poem, of Wilde's own volume, a value that does not belong to much that lies between. That Beethoven's *Ninth Symphony* or Michael Angelo's *Creation of Adam* has no more and no other kind of æsthetic value, than a perfect piece of porcelain or a bit of arabesque adornment, is simply absurd. It was all very well to react against Ruskin, who erred quite as grievously on the other side; but that Wilde's error was the more perilous, is evident in his own work, as well as in his career.

WITH great insight and large objective vision, Wilde wilfully sacrificed both for brilliant paradoxes. He preferred an epigram to truth, and a startling, beautiful sentence to a sanely balanced thought. There could be no clearer evidence of his paradox than that his discussion of socialism converts it into pure anarchism. He surprises, stimulates, delights; but it is champagne, not the nourishing food of the intellect, and leaves one with little beyond a metaphorical headache. The pity is that such talent and so fine a style should be used to so slight an end.

Irish Poetry

WILD, wierd and wistful,
　　Watered with weary weeping,
Woven of wasteful winds,
Whispering wonderful woe;

Lightly lilting with laughter,
Lingering long over love-notes,
Languid with lonely longing,
Lifted with light of love;

Singing songs of the Siren,
Shadowed with somberous sorrows,
Soft as a sigh out of slumber——
Such is sweet Irish song.

Beads From The Rosary Of Life

TAKE pearls of Love and string them on a thread of Wisdom, and you have the Rosary of Life, to which every prayer is a human tear.

The spiritual universe is an infinite circle, of which every soul is the center, and whose unknown circumference is God.

Light cast by the fires of martyrdom may make men see, even as sunlight: the one need is that they should see.

Human lives: wind-blown bubbles, on the breast of the ocean of Time; yet with all the meaning of Eternity in their transient being!

Great thinking is like sunlight: it reveals itself. You do not need to prove the sun is shining: open your eyes and see. So truth carries its own warrant, once it is expressed.

Ideals are not safe; Prudence rightly dreads them. If you hitch your wagon to a star, you must expect a wild journey, with numerous accidents on the Milky Way.

He who always laughs at himself is a fool; he who never laughs at himself is a hopeless bigot.

Take the soil of Desire and let the sun of Love shine on it; then water it with the tears of Suffering; and you will have a harvest of which every grain is a gem of Truth, and each leaf a new page in God's revelation.

One questions, at times, whether anyone really lives except the true artist. The answer is, everyone should be an artist in the marble from the quarry of life.

Whole truths never scintillate. The narrower a half-truth, the more brilliantly its cleverly-cut facets shine.

Jealousy is a by-product of the possessive instinct.

Love never possesses, except in entire freedom, where the other gives inevitably and gladly: hardest of lessons to learn and live!

Possession as property, and the mutual possession of love, are in different worlds; and are, indeed, as reciprocally exclusive as love and jealousy: where one is, to that extent the other is not.

Love is never *changeless*; but it may be eternal, in an ever-growing process to which there is no end.

To have adequate resource in one's own spirit is a mark of the highest cultivation, and is one secret of wise and serene living.

To put repose into the spirit of the day, and yet get the day's work done: that is the need.

He who conquers hate and the spirit of revenge, in his own breast, is free and master of the tyrant that wrongs him.

One danger of success is the temptation to repeat oneself, instead of pressing on to new achievement. To travel over and over the same road is to dig the ruts ever deeper.

A rebellion is a revolt against established authority; a revolution is such a revolt successfully concluded. Every victorious rebellion, History records as a revolution; every unsuccessful revolution, as a rebellion: History does not go behind the returns.

Ignorance is the bulwark of despotism; education is the lever of democracy.

A superstition is a belief in what does not exist. If its object is proved to exist, the belief was not superstition and was falsely so called.

Injustice in high places is possible only because there is evil in the breast of man. Overthrowing the tyrant is but the initial step of emancipation: until the common heart is cleansed of hate, the external tyrant in some form will return.

How reality fades into illusion, and life is arrayed in dreams. Things pass; but thoughts remain—rocks in the ocean. To live well, even within the dream: that is the secret.

Creation of beauty that incarnates truth is the one achievement of the human spirit in itself worth while; as the wisdom recognizing the truth and the love appreciating the beauty are the ultimate ends of the inner life.

To accept life, without yielding to superstitious conventionality on the one hand, nor to vulgar licentiousness on the other; not to mistake sexual curiosity for love, nor selfish caprices for loyalty to self: that is the personal problem of the new age.

To A. C. G.

[For her birthday, April 21, 1919]

DEAR, my daughter, you are fair and
    sweet and lovely,
  The hard awkward years are past;
My heart rests in you without the old for-
    boding,
For I know your new awakened aim will last.

In your face a haunting likeness to your
    mother,
  The same movement in your walk:
How you flood my heart with memories and
    echoes,
When you come into my study for a talk!

Fair with promise, your life opens out before
    you,
  You can climb the sun-lit height;
Faith and hope and aspiration beckon upward,
Where the mountain summits flame in morning
    light.

236

While for me the tide ebbs out, the shadows
    deepen,
  Down the valley drifts the mist;
Through the trees a bird-call echoes in the
    twilight;
In the nest, his mate in silence waits the tryst.

Youth and love and faith!   Dear, keep them
    fresh for always;
  Share the joy and ease the pain;
Do the service that will help another onward:
Only thus will life its dearest joy attain.

May the years bring added grace and deep-
    ened wisdom—
  All the answer to your heart;
Till you learn of love and life the full fruition;
Meet the challenge, find your task and do
    your part!

THE MYSTERY OF LIFE

[Morgantown, West Va., June 24, 1909]

THE mystery of human life broods ever more sombrely over one's mind. What is it all for—the countless lives that come and pass, apparently merely to eat, sleep and propagate their kind—the fierce struggle just to get through life with sufficient food, clothing and shelter? Is it worth while? The deeper human relationships and the discipline of character are unconscious corollaries for so many. Certainly, a larger synthesis, than that of these feverish years, is necessary to give meaning to the chapter of life we can see. How many go through life without ever being born; and if they are never to be born, what is the use? Certainly, all experience and observation of life drive one increasingly to a spiritual interpretation of it, in terms of eternity—or to despair.

[Vredeoord, May 30, 1914]

THE illusions of Space and Time defeat life. Always we think that somewhere else, at some other time, we should feel the great inspiration, accomplish the creative action. Thus we go on excusing ourselves, blaming circumstances and so weakening the will, until life slips through our fingers and is gone. Illusion—pure illusion! Ceaseless effort is mediocrity; evaded effort is self-deception; rightly balanced effort is the key to genius. To drive oneself with relentless will; to let go and respond with open, care-free mind and heart: these, together, are great living; either, unbalanced, leads to bankruptcy.

[Muskogee, Okla., June 19, 1921]

NATURE is prodigal with color, as with all else. The sun sank behind the low hill, above which was a wide azure band; while, higher, were compact masses of feathery clouds. A few moments after the sun was gone, these cloud masses were aflame with red and gold. Slowly the color changed and faded, until just the edge of the azure was alight. Gradually all faded into darkness. Now, with the clouds dark gray, the azure band has softly become gold.

O prolific Nature, painter of dawns and sunsets, wearer of the blue garment sewn with silver stars, creator of living and ever changing beauty, covering the earth with a living green mantle, pouring out lives innumerable as stars: O Artist, Mother, Mystery!

Age

SLOWLY the tide ebbs out,
    'Neath the leaden gray sky;
A flash of white wing, yellow beak,
And a harsh sea-gull's cry;
A bit of wreckage, half-loosed, in the sand,
A broken spar drifting by,
    Then the night!

THE THREE DIMENSIONS

[Twin Mountain, N. H., July 27, 1906]

AS with all else we know, there are three dimensions to the human spirit—height, breadth and depth. Characters such as St. Francis and Jesus are marked by spiritual height; Dante and Browning are characterized by depth of personality; while such men as Goethe and Shakespeare show the greatest breadth in relation to the objective world. The appreciation of one type should not blind us to the value of the others.

[June 19, 1921]

IT is thought that transcends space and out-runs time. It is thought that conceives the infinite and the eternal. Should the material universe prove to be finite, the thought universe would remain infinite and the world of matter would be included in it as a fragment.

243

MUSIC AND THE SPIRIT

[Oklahoma City, February 6, 1922]

WHY is it that certain strains of music search so profoundly the heart: wakening blurred memories of dead yesterdays—of voices long silent and dim-moving hands that are dust: like the perfume of dead roses, acrid and sweet? Chords of emotion vibrate to chords of memory; and the sarcophagus cells of the brain resurrect their dead. O mystery beyond mystery! There are moods when life and death blend, like form and close-clinging shadow.

An Old Dedication

FROM my heart these thoughts I wreathe,
      To thine they go;
The love and life that in them breathe,
   Thou dost know,
   Alone dost know.

Some are white, with radiance clear
   As driven snow;
Some are crimsoned, with heart's dear
   Blood they flow,
   Life's blood they flow.

These are all a token slight,
   Dearest fair,
A wreath of flowers, red and white,
   Thou mayst wear,
   For thee to wear.

These I lay in worship pure
   At thy feet;
Symbols of a love, life-sure:
   An offering meet,
   For thy soul meet.

INDEX

"A. C. G., To" 236, 237
Aeschylus, 93
Age, 16, 196, 241
"Age," 241
"Alone," 113
American life, 11, 21, 123, 124, 136, 137, 141, 144-149, 155, 156, 197, 201, 204, 205, 226, 227
Angelico, Fra, 81
Angelo, Michael, 80, 81, 88, 89, 92, 93, 134, 228
Art : of Jules Guérin, 51; modern, 55, 56; of Brangwyn, 55, 56; of Florence, 80, 81 ; of Luca della Robbia, 80, 81 ; of Michael Angelo, 80, 88, 89; of Raphael, 85-87; and Nature, 117; of Rodin, 134; American, 155, 156; realism in, 177; and life, 219; for art's sake, 228; of music, 244
Assisi, 82-84
Aurelius, Marcus, 102-104
Autumn, 160
"Autumn in Everything," 106
"Awakening," 225

"Beads from the Rosary of Life," 231–235
Beethoven, 93, 228
Bernhardt, 161
Bonds, 7, 183
Botticelli, 81
Brangwyn, Frank, 55, 56
Browning, 93, 193, 201, 242
Brunelleschi, 81
Bruno, Giordano, 94-97

California, 48, 50-58, 74
"Call of Arcady, The," 115, 116
"Christmas Eve," 173
"City, The," 207, 208
Compensations, 215
Competition, 59
Conduct of life, 7, 8, 9, 13, 27, 123, 126, 164, 168, 175, 183, 206, 219, 231-235, 239
Coöperation, 137
"Cost, The," 140
Culture, the index of, 27
"Cup of the Darker Drink, The," 142, 143

Dante, 38, 81, 190, 192, 193, 201, 242
"Dejection," 43
Democracy, 129, 137, 144,

145, 149-153, 186, 188, 204, 205, 234
"Did She But Know," 61
Drama of life, the, 5
Dramatic Monologues: "Erasmus," 66-69; "Giordano Bruno," 94-97; "Marcus Aurelius," 102-104; "The Lost Cause," 202, 203

"Edinburgh Castle," 199, 200
Emerson, 18, 19, 107, 108, 171, 197, 198
English Cemetery in Rome, 98
Erasmus, 64, 66-69
"Erasmus," 66-69
Esoteric, the, 216

Faith, 21, 221
"Field Flowers," 162, 163
Florence, 80, 81
"Four Faces," 88-91
France, the old régime in, 75, 76, 209, 210
Francis, Saint of Assisi, 83, 84, 242
Frederick the Great, 64, 65
Freedom, 7
French literature, 221
Frontier life, 176
"Fulfillment," 30

Gautier, 187
"Gethsemane," 110

"Giordano Bruno," 94-97
Giotto, 81
Goethe, 18, 32, 39, 40, 42, 107, 165, 169-172, 177, 201, 219, 242; Werther, 169, 170; Italian Journey, 171, 172
Government: centralized, 186, 204; paternalism in, 188; propaganda of opinions by, 204
Grand Canyon, 45-47, 50
"Gray is the Sky," 125
Great Salt Lake, 28
Guérin, Jules, 51

Hearn, Lafcadio, 189
"Heart O' Mine," 132, 133
"Her Kiss," 191
"Hope of Spring, the" 120
Human factor, the, 185
Human wreckage, 62, 63
Humor, 206, 232

Ibsen, 31-42, 222; Peer Gynt, 31, 32; The Doll's House, 33; Ghosts, 33, 34; Rosmersholm, 34; Hedda Gabler, 35; Little Eyolf, 36, 37; truth to life of, 37, 38; women of, 38, 39; life of, 39; teaching of, 40; characterization of, 40-42
Ideas, permanent versus transient, 8, 15
Illusions, 239

Intellectual life, 8, 15, 16, 59, 60, 70, 101, 126, 164, 197, 216, 226, 231-235, 243
"Irish Poetry," 230
"Italy Called," 99, 100
"Italy Calls," 77-79

Jerome, Saint, 165, 166
Jesus, 242
Judging lives, 219
Julius II, 92

"Lady of Lake Lucerne, The," 178-182
Leadership, 150, 151, 227
Life, human: mystery of, 5, 20, 44, 174, 238, 244; useless freedom in, 7; problem of, 9, 174, 231, 238; wreckage of, 62, 63; power of recovery in, 131; adaptability of, 136; the one reality, 157; interpretation of, in art, 177; relations in, 183, 232, 233; centering in every place, 195; adjustments in, 215; three dimensions in, 242
"Life Stake, The," 218
"Lincoln," 148
Literature, current, 12, 123, 220, 221
Living the present moment, 9, 126, 164, 234, 235, 239

"Lost Cause, The," 202, 203
Loti, Pierre, 212, 213
Louys, Pierre, 118, 119
"Love Song, A", 49
Lowell, 193

Maeterlinck, 18, 19
"Marcus Aurelius," 102-104
"Memory of Mrs. J. E. M., In," 214
Modesty, 127
Moods, need to control, 13
Moore, George, 187
Mozart, 93
Music and the Spirit, 244

Napoleon, 126, 227
Nature, intelligence in, 20, 44; ministry of, 22, 23, 74, 111, 112, 240; beauty of, 109, 111, 240; and art, 117
Nebraska, 74
"Nightfall," 17
Novels, modern, 12

Odin, Illinois, 195
"Old Dedication, An," 245
Opportunity, 164

Panama-Pacific Exposition 50-58
"Parting," 167
"Plains, The," 122
Plato, 149, 171, 197

Poems: "Song," 6; "The Ship," 10; "Nightfall," 17; "The Rocky Mountains," 24-26; "Fulfillment," 30; "Dejection," 43; "A Love Song," 49; "Did She But Know," 61; "Erasmus," 66-69; "Italy Calls," 77-79; "Sunset at Assisi," 82-84; "Four Faces," 88-91; "Giordano Bruno," 94-97; "Italy Called," 99-100; "Marcus Aurelius," 102-104; "Autumn in Everything," 106; "Gethsemane," 110; "Alone," 113; "The Call of Arcady," 115, 116, "The Hope of Spring," 120; "The Plains," 122; "Gray is the Sky," 125; "Sunday in the City," 128; "Heart O' Mine," 132, 133; "Unity," 135; "The Cost," 140; "The Cup of the Darker Drink," 142, 143; "Lincoln," 148; "Spring," 154; "A Sunset on Lake Ontario," 158, 159; "Field Flowers," 162-163; "Parting," 167; "Christmas Eve," 173; "The Lady of Lake Lucerne," 178-182; "What is in Your Hearts, My Children?," 184; "Her Kiss," 191; "With Some Carnations," 194; "Edinburgh Castle," 199, 200; "The Lost Cause," 202, 203; "The City," 207, 208; "A Thunder Shower," 211; "In Memory of Mrs. J. E. M.," 214; "The Life-Stake," 218; "Awakening," 225; "Irish Poetry," 230; "To A. C. G.," 236, 237; "Age," 241; "An Old Dedication," 245

Progress, 11, 15, 16, 27, 59, 60, 72, 73, 136, 137, 150, 151, 185, 224

Radicals, 72, 73
Raphael, 81, 85-87, 88, 92, 93
Reconstruction, 11, 141, 146, 147, 185, 201, 204, 205, 210, 224; program of, 224
Red River Canyon, 121
Repose of spirit, 126, 141, 164, 220, 233
Revolution, 65, 75, 76, 234
Robbia, Luca della, 80, 81
Rocky Mountains, 22-26, 29
"Rocky Mountains, The," 24-26
Rodin, 134
Rosary of Life, the, 231-235
Ruskin, 228

Sacrifice, effect of, 136, 137
Saint-Simon, Mémoires, 75, 76
Sarto, Andrea del, 81, 85 90, 91
Savonarola, 81
Schiller, 18
Schnitzler, Arthur, 14
Shakespeare, 42, 177, 192, 201, 222, 223, 242
Shaw Bernard, 152, 153
"Ship, The," 10
Sistine Madonna, 85-87
Sociology, modern, 12, 16, 188
Socrates, 152, 153
"Song," 6
Sophocles, 93
Southwest, the, 124
"Spring," 154
Student spirit, 226
"Sunday in the City," 128
"Sunset at Assisi," 82-84
"Sunset on Lake Ontario, A," 158, 159

Teaching, 71
Tennyson, 93, 193
Thoreau, 107, 108, 183
Thought, universe of, 243
"Thunder Shower, A," 211
Toleration, 27
Travel, 101
Truth and Opinion, 8

"Unity," 135

Venus worship, 118, 119, 187
Vinci, Leonardo da, 85, 89, 90
Voltaire, 64, 65
Voss, 18

Wagner, 219
War, the, 129-131, 136-141, 144-147, 185, 201, 209, 210; fundamental issue in, 130; America and the War, 136-141, 144-147
Washington, D. C., 155, 156
West, the, 21
"What is in Your Hearts, My Children?" 184
White Mountains, the, 105, 109, 111, 112, 114
Whitman, 42
Wilde, Oscar, 118, 228, 229
Will, the, 168
Wilson, President, 210
Wisdom, 8, 73, 164, 231, 235
"With Some Carnations," 194
Women: worship of, 189; mediæval cult of, 190; influence of, 217; the lot of, 217
Work, 175, 219

Youth, 11, 16, 146, 147, 196, 226; in the present age, 11; view of, 16; quick recovery in, 146; and age, 196

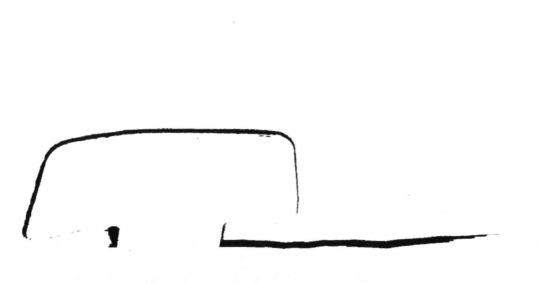

Im The Story
personalised classic books

JANE
IN
WONDERLAND

LEWIS
CARROLL

"Beautiful gift.. lovely finish.
My Niece loves it, so precious!"

Helen R Brumfieldon

⭐⭐⭐⭐⭐

**UNIQUE
GIFT**

FOR KIDS, PARTNERS
AND FRIENDS

Timeless books such as:

Kids

Alice in Wonderland · The Jungle Book · The Wonderful Wizard of Oz
Peter and Wendy · Robin Hood · The Prince and The Pauper
The Railway Children · Treasure Island · A Christmas Carol

Adults

Romeo and Juliet · Dracula

Highly
Customizable

Change
Books Title

Replace
Characters Names
with yours

Upload
Photo for
inside page

Add
Inscriptions

Visit
Im The Story .com
and order yours today!